A Path with a Heart

ERICKSONIAN UTILIZATION
WITH RESISTANT AND
CHRONIC CLIENTS

A Path with a Heart

ERICKSONIAN UTILIZATION WITH RESISTANT AND CHRONIC CLIENTS

By

YVONNE M. DOLAN

BRUNNER/MAZEL *Publishers* • New York

Library of Congress Cataloging-in-Publication Data

Dolan, Yvonne M.
  A path with a heart.

  Bibliography: p.
  Includes index.
    1. Psychotherapist and patient.   2. Resistance
(Psychoanalysis)   3. Hypnotism—Therapeutic use.
4. Psychotherapy.   I. Erickson, Milton H.   II. Title.
III. Title: Ericksonian utilization with resistant and
chronic clients. [DNLM: 1. Hypnosis—methods.
2. Psychotherapy—methods. WM 415 D659P]
RC480.8.D65   1985   616.89'162   85-4225
ISBN 0-87630-718-7

Published by
BRUNNER/MAZEL, INC.
19 Union Square West
New York, New York 10003

Manufactured in the United States of America

10 9 8 7 6 5 4 3 2 1

This book is dedicated to Charlie Johnson, a very skilled psychotherapist who has integrity, a wonderful sense of curiosity, and a twinkle in his eyes. I've never heard him refer to anyone as ''resistant'' or ''chronic.''

Foreword

Historically, hypnotherapy has been assiduously avoided in the treatment of psychotics. One of the myths that pervades both the professional and lay communities is that hypnosis is too all-powerful—that it can precipitate psychosis in patients with "fragile egos."

This myth was disproved by Milton Erickson, the master psychiatrist whose extensive work with hypnotherapy is the basis for Yvonne Dolan's work on the treatment of chronic patients, *A Path with a Heart*. Erickson was the first practitioner to consistently demonstrate the efficacy of formal and informal hypnotherapy with schizophrenics, and now Dolan has advanced Erickson's naturalistic techniques with her eminently readable exposition of practical, commonsense techniques.

Erickson's "naturalistic approach"—a method of treatment he developed and named—is hypnosis without a formal induction. In general, Ericksonian hypnotherapy is a method par excellence of influence communication whereby all patient behaviors are utilized as resources to gain the patient's cooperation. Ericksonian techniques include both formal and informal inductions. Hypnosis without an induction is particularly useful in dealing with resistance.

Focusing naturalistic techniques on the treatment of chronics and psychotics, as Dolan does in the present work, is something Erickson himself would have approved of. These are among the most resistant patients in psychotherapy, and therefore are keenly suited to techniques that elicit their cooperation. Unfortunately, the pairing of chronics and psychotics in terms of treatment needs, although making good sense, has often been overlooked in the literature. It is good to have it emphasized here.

This book is one of the first by a second-generation Ericksonian. Dolan never met Milton Erickson. Instead she learned hypnosis by reading and studying with some of Erickson's disciples—and she learned well. Her techniques are readily applicable for both the novice and experienced therapist. Especially valuable is the seven-step method for metaphor construction. Also refreshing is Dolan's emphasis on the therapist's well-being: her presentation of what therapists can do to change their personal attitudes and behaviors, thereby helping themselves to avoid burnout. She provides methods for therapists, especially those working with chronic patients, to become more comfortable and optimistic.

This is not a book for dogmatic family therapists or those who subscribe to the theory of "better living through chemistry." Dolan does not parrot party line, but draws from various sources in the development of her personal style. In the tradition of R.D. Laing, her orientation takes an interactional perspective on the determinants of schizophrenic behavior. Following Erickson, she emphasizes case studies to point out commonsense techniques that are effective in modifying behavior. And then she extends Erickson's contributions in her own original way, all the while maintaining the essential Ericksonian philosophy of an individualized, client-centered hypnotherapy.

Reading this book reminded me of the first three cases that Erickson discussed with me when I met him in 1973. These were examples of naturalistic techniques with both psychotic and resistant patients, and at first the stories bewildered me. I didn't know exactly what Erickson was trying to say.

At the time, I was a novice therapist interested in working with schizophrenics, and the first case he told me about was a patient with whom he had limited success (Zeig, 1980). Then he told me a second fragment about a psychotic patient named Jimmy. (This was unusual; in his teaching tales it was commonly Erickson's style to limit his discussion to complete and successful cases, not to provide examples through case fragments.) Erickson told me that at the turn of the century Jimmy was admitted to the hospital with a diagnosis of chronic idiocy. Thirty years later he was still in the hospital. His life consisted of walking around the grounds collecting "treasures," such as rocks and bits of paper.

One day there was a small fire on the ward and Jimmy rose to the occasion, taking charge when the two orderlies froze in panic. Jimmy told one of the attendants to take the patients outside, and then he took the other attendant around the ward, checking room by room to ensure that all of the patients were safe. Erickson returned to the hospital shortly after the fire had been extinguished and found that Jimmy had reverted to his precrisis state. Erickson asked him about his actions during the fire, but Jimmy couldn't remember what happened. He knew something had happened, but he couldn't say what.

Erickson had presented this story by looking at me pensively and saying, "To assume something about a patient is awfully wrong." I often remind myself that the story of Jimmy was one of the first lessons he wanted to teach me. He often criticized preconceived theoretical models as limiting the practitioner.

The third case that Erickson discussed involved a woman psychopath whom he refused to treat. He told me he didn't know anyone he hated enough to whom he could refer her for psychotherapy.

As you might imagine, I was amazed by Erickson's stories. I had come to him because he was the world's most successful therapist, and two of the first three cases he discussed were patients whom he didn't treat—one schizophrenic and the other a resistant psychopath.

Gradually I began to realize that Erickson's therapeutic method was based on the importance of the patient's response to the communication; he deemphasized technique. He was telling me that not every patient can be cured and not every patient is a candidate for psychotherapy. If there is no responsiveness, there is no therapy—no matter how creative the therapist's technique.

These lessons are the foundation of the techniques described in this clear and concise book by an obviously talented therapist. *A Path with a Heart* provides an orientation through which clinicians may pump new life into their therapeutic approach.

To resist its important message would be awfully wrong.

Jeffrey K. Zeig, Ph.D.
Director
The Milton H. Erickson Foundation

REFERENCE

Zeig, J. K. (Ed.). *A teaching seminar with Milton H. Erickson.* New York: Brunner/ Mazel, 1980.

Contents

Acknowledgments

There are several people who deserve special thanks for their help in making this book possible:

My husband, Charlie Johnson, provided untiring support, well-timed humor, and helpful professional criticism, and he taught me how to use a word processor.

Stephen Gilligan and Paul Carter, in their excellent training workshops on Ericksonian hypnotherapy, were the catalysts for a series of enjoyable personal and professional learnings, many of which are reflected in the book's content.

Jeffrey Zeig provided advice and encouragement, as well as clarification of key issues about Ericksonian utilization through his excellent training lectures on Dr. Erickson's work.

Mary Jane Wollenberg helped me to understand the wonderful potential in using occupational therapy activities as part of Ericksonian interventions with chronically mentally ill clients.

Long, thoughtful conversations with the following people between 1979 and 1984 were especially valuable for sorting out general concepts that are at the heart of the Ericksonian utilization approach:

David Bice, Linda Mraz, Ellen Solloway, Gene Combs, Jill Freedman, Maxine Bernard Shear, and Michael Westcott.

I am grateful to John Rosen for his kind support and the loan of his deluxe typewriter when the book was in its earliest stages.

I would also like to thank my editor at Brunner/Mazel, Ann Alhadeff, who provided helpful suggestions and made the publication process a very pleasant experience.

Finally, I am especially grateful to my clients who, over the past 10 years, have graciously allowed me to learn from them and in many cases have kept in touch after their therapy has ended.

Introduction

I did not have the privilege of knowing Milton H. Erickson. My admiration and appreciation of his work grew from careful study of his books, collected papers, and tape-recorded transcripts, as well as from observing the work of his former students.

My involvement with "chronic" and "resistant" clients began with a student internship. This was followed by eight years of direct clinical work with individuals and groups in community mental health settings, eventually encompassing consultation to inpatient units, group homes, nursing homes, sheltered workshops, day treatment programs, outreach organizations, social service agencies, supervision of student interns, clinicians, technicians and other front-line service providers.

I first began to apply Ericksonian techniques to chronic and "resistant" clients while working as the director of a small adult day psychiatric program located, coincidentally, in Juneau, Wisconsin, the county where Milton Erickson grew up on his father's farm. The clients I saw there were mostly from the local farm community. Their frankness and obvious good common sense deeply impressed me and gave me a strong sense of responsibility as a therapist. Working with this client population from the Wisconsin farm community, I began to particularly appreciate the good "salt of the earth" flavor that shines through Erickson's allusions to his early personal learning experience.

WHY THIS BOOK WAS WRITTEN

This book was written to provide practical therapeutic alternatives for therapists who work with chronic and resistant clients in community outpatient, day hospital and psychiatric inpatient settings. It is written particularly for the therapist who constantly seeks to refine and expand his or her therapeutic skills.

Chronic and resistant clients are a challenging learning resource for both the seasoned and beginning clinician. These clients have generally had years of therapy experience in the context of their symptomatology and will demand an exquisite level of rapport and precise intervention techniques in order to respond therapeutically.

Definition of Terms

For the purposes of this book, "chronic" refers specifically to those individuals who have been involved in the mental health treatment system for three or more years without symptomatic relief.

"Chronicity" refers to a pattern of repeated psychiatric inpatient hospitalizations, and the client's apparent need for continuing mental health services for an undetermined length of time in the future.

"Resistance" refers to any behavior on the part of the client that appears to be getting in the way of the desired therapeutic outcome.

I have chosen to combine the discussion of chronic and resistant clients in this book because these two client groups share a number of similarities and are related to each other on a continuum of symptoms and duration. For example, a chronic client is, in effect, a very experienced resistant client who has succeeded in resisting over the months and years and, consequently, has continued to suffer symptoms. Without successful therapeutic intervention, today's resistant clients become tomorrow's chronic clients. Resistant clients are at risk for chronicity.

"Utilization" is the process of incorporating the client's ongoing and symptomatic behavior and perceptions into the therapeutic change process.

Erickson's utilization approach to trance induction (1958, 1959) and his utilization of the client's presenting behavior as an integral part of therapy (1955, 1965) are among his most important original contributions to the fields of psychotherapy and clinical hypnosis (Erickson, Rossi, & Rossi, 1976). While the utilization techniques described in this book will often result in clients developing hypnotic trances, the specific focus will be the utilization of the client's current behavior and perceptions in the therapeutic change process. A comprehensive account of Erickson's hypnotic techniques is beyond the scope of this or any single volume.

The material in this book is presented in such a manner that concepts and techniques are developed sequentially. It is therefore recommended that the chapters be read in numerical order. For the reader's convenience, an overview of the contents of this book follows.

Chapter 1, The Complexity of Working with Chronic and Resistant Clients, examines the complexity of working with this client population. Therapeutic requirements for success are described within the context of Erickson's values of pragmatism, integrity, and precision.

Chapter 2, The Nature of Ericksonian Utilization, defines the concept of Ericksonian utilization. Requirements for successful utilization are listed and discussed in specific terms. Two case examples, one from Erickson and one from the author, are included.

Chapter 3, A Naturalistic Perspective for Hypnotic Trance, provides a naturalistic perspective for clients' hypnotic experiences in the context of Ericksonian utilization. Examples are provided for each hypnotic phenomenon. Therapeutic advantages of the trance state are explained. Guidelines are given for therapeutically utilizing the trance states that are likely to occur as a result of the utilization techniques described in subsequent chapters. Special attention is given to the subject of hypnosis with psychotic clients.

Chapter 4, Bypassing Conscious Blocks Through Interspersal and Presuppositions, defines and explains the use of interspersal and presuppositions with the habitually nonresponsive client. A series of simple and effective formulae for presuppositions is provided. Erickson's interspersal approach is discussed in detail, with a case excerpt provided for illustration. Practical suggestions are offered for therapists wishing to strengthen the effectiveness of their delivery style when employing interspersal techniques with specific clients. A case example is included in which the combined use of presuppositions and interspersal techniques is demonstrated.

Chapter 5, "Yes" Sets and "No" Sets, enables the therapist to recognize and utilize "yes" sets and "no" sets. Prerequisites for developing an acceptance set ("yes" set) are defined. Practical instructions are supplied for employing truisms and compound suggestions to develop a therapeutic "yes" set. The therapist is given a step-by-step formula for transforming the "no" set into a "yes" set when working with resistant clients. Guidelines are provided to enable the therapist to recognize and utilize the moment at which the "no" set becomes a "yes" set. Case excerpts and case examples are provided.

Chapter 6, Strategies for Communicating Acceptance in an Undeniable Way, focuses on symbolic verbal and nonverbal communication techniques designed to fit the specific needs of chronic and resistant clients. Concepts are illustrated with a case example describing Erickson's work with a chronic psychiatric patient.

Chapter 7, Establishing New Therapeutic Resources Through Associational Cues, defines and explains the therapeutic use of associational cues with chronic and resistant clients. Examples are provided to enable the therapist to utilize clients' existing, naturalistic associational cues to develop new therapeutic resources. Direct and indirect strategies are explained in detail with guidelines provided to enable the therapist to individualize techniques to fit specific clients. A case example is included.

Chapter 8, Reframing Chronic Symptoms—A Utilization Approach, illustrates and explains the direct and indirect use of associational cues in a reframing intervention. The concept of reframing is defined and explained. A five-step formula is provided for utilizing associational cues to therapeutically reframe problematic behaviors and perceptions. The five-step formula is illustrated with a case example of a catatonic client.

Chapter 9, Metaphors: Communicating with Chronic and Resistant Clients Through Stories, discusses the metaphorical aspects of clients' communication. A step-by-step model is provided with guidelines to enable the therapist to construct effective therapeutic metaphors for specific chronic or resistant clients.

Chapter 10, Using Metaphors with Psychotic Clients, explains the therapeutic purposes of telling a metaphor to a psychotic client. Practical considerations and specific guidelines are provided for creating therapeutic metaphors for use with psychotic and semi-psychotic clients.

Chapter 11, Changing Chronic Problem Behaviors into Therapeutic Resources, focuses on the treatment of long-term problematic behaviors through utilization techniques. A list of assessment questions is provided to help the therapist identify aspects of existing behavior that can be utilized to lead to therapeutic change. Two case examples are presented to illustrate the process of designing utilization interventions for clients with chronic problem behaviors.

Chapter 12, Ericksonian Utilization in Group Settings, focuses on the group setting as therapeutic resource. Techniques for adapting Ericksonian strategies to group settings are outlined and illustrated with two case histories.

Chapter 13, The Therapist as an Instrument, explores therapist and co-therapist roles in an Ericksonian perspective. A series of practical suggestions are provided for use in cases where the therapist feels "stuck." Also included are strategies designed to maintain and enhance the therapist's comfort and creativity when dealing with especially difficult clients. Ericksonian techniques particularly suited to co-therapy situations are described in detail.

The Appendix contains a Metaphor Worksheet form, for use in designing therapeutic metaphors, and a Paradoxical Attendance Contract, for use as an intervention with chronic clients who seek but typically fail to show up for therapy. Also included is a Reframing Worksheet, for use in gathering information that is helpful for designing effective reframing interventions for problem behaviors.

The author believes that most individuals who go to the trouble of becoming therapists do so because of genuine concern for other human beings. Therefore, the following material is offered with the implicit assumption that the reader already possesses the integrity and potential ability to deeply appreciate the self and others that is so much a hallmark and crucial precondition for the Ericksonian utilization approach. For the therapist willing to bring the best parts of his or her humanity and future learning to the therapeutic endeavor, Ericksonian utilization truly offers a ''path with a heart.''

1

The Complexity of Working with Chronic and Resistant Clients

"Chronic" and "resistant" are two labels that can contribute to demoralization on the part of both therapist and client. Even if these terms are not directly voiced to the client, their presence is likely to be felt in the therapist's demeanor and nonverbal communication.

To the extent that therapists blindly accept the terms "resistant" and "chronic" as accurate current descriptions of the client, they will further contribute to the difficulty the client is experiencing. "Chronic" is actually a comment on the therapeutic community's long-term inability to effectively treat the client. "Resistant" is a comment on the therapeutic relationship and indicates the extent to which the therapist has been unsuccessful in accepting, communicating, and achieving trust with the client.

A MUCH-NEEDED PERSPECTIVE OF OPTIMISM

In order to succeed with "chronic" and "resistant" clients, the therapist must let go of the demoralization and negative expectations attached to those labels and develop an expectation of positive outcome.

1

Ericksonian utilization, with its inherent perspective of optimism and nonjudgmental posture, offers an antidote for the demoralization that handicaps therapists working with clients labeled chronic and resistant. The Ericksonian perspective emphasizes the value of symptomatic problems first being acknowledged and accepted, then utilized as therapeutic resources to lead the client to choose more rewarding behaviors and perceptions.

THERAPISTS WHO TREAT CHRONIC AND RESISTANT CLIENTS

The earliest years of many therapists' careers are spent seeing the clients whom the more experienced therapists choose not to see. It is an odd bit of irony about our mental health system that the most difficult clients are not infrequently given to the most inexperienced therapists.

There are some treatment advantages in assigning chronic and resistant clients to interns and novice therapists. What the novice therapist and intern frequently lack in experience and skill they sometimes make up for in optimism and enthusiasm, attitudes valuable in working with chronic and recalcitrant clients.

All too often a seasoned therapist will tell a novice not to become overly involved with the client. While this is technically accurate advice, a highly personalized and perhaps extreme measure is likely to be required in the case of most clients who have been labeled chronic. "Commonsense" and "common" therapeutic methods have already failed this client. Otherwise the chronic individual would not now be the person described in a five-inch thick treatment file with a ten-year history of recurrent inpatient psychiatric admissions.

Conversely, it is well known among experienced clinicians that rigidly expecting a client to change at the therapist's rate, rather than according to the client's own internal rhythms and personal abilities, is tantamount to setting that person up to fail. The over-eager, enthusiastic, naive graduate intern may, if not warned, fall into the idealistic abyss of setting out to single-handedly empty the psychiatric units in short order. At worst, the overidealistic and zealous fledgling clinician may encounter an experience analogous to that of the man who tries to help a butterfly emerge from its cocoon.

The man, impatient with the butterfly's slow progress in "struggling" out of the cocoon, seeks to help the creature. He fails to recognize the protective nature of the constricting "resistant" cocoon. The butterfly, with the man's "help," is set free in the cold air prematurely. Deprived of adequate time to make the necessary adjustments within the cocoon, it crumbles into a helpless suffering heap. The therapist must have reverence and appreciation for each client's personal rate of change, idiosyncrasies, difficulties, vulnerabilities, and resources.

On the other hand, if the therapist goes too far in the direction of avoiding stress in the interest of protecting a vulnerable client, he or she risks depriving the client of the very motivational factors that are needed for recovery.

In working with chronic and resistant clients, the path between these two extremes is sometimes very narrow. Clearly, good intentions are not enough! The skilled therapist needs much more.

In order to be effective, the therapist who works with chronic and resistant clients must find a way to preserve an initial perspective of confidence in the client's ability to respond favorably to treatment, while simultaneously seeing beyond the myopic oversimplifications that may plague and hamper the unseasoned therapist. This is no simple task.

THE THERAPEUTIC RELEVANCE OF INTEGRITY

In the demanding context of working with chronic and resistant clients, the Ericksonian approach offers much-needed values of pragmatism coupled with integrity and precision. Erickson viewed the "resistant" behavior as one more aspect of the client's symptomatology and devised precise strategies to utilize that symptomatology to lead to therapeutic change.

Therapists wishing to help their patients should never scorn, condemn, or reject any part of a patient's conduct simply because it is obstructive, unreasonable, or even irrational. The patient's behavior is part of the problem that brought him into the office; it constitutes the personal environment within which the therapy must take effect; it may constitute the dominant force in the total patient-doctor relationship. Since whatever patients bring into the office is in some way both a part of them and a part of their problem, the patient should be viewed with a sympathetic eye appraising the totality which confronts the therapist. (Erickson, 1965, in *Collected Papers, Vol. 1*, p. 213)

Erickson emphasized the quality of the relationship between therapist and client while viewing the client as a total human personality rather than simply a set of lingering diagnoses or symptoms. Earlier in the above quoted article, he states:

In dealing with any type of patient clinically, there is a most important consideration that should be kept constantly in mind. That is that the patient's needs as a human personality should be an ever-present question for the therapist to insure recognition at each manifestation. Merely to make a correct diagnosis of the illness and to know the correct method of treatment is not enough. Fully as important is that the patient be receptive of the therapy and cooperative in regard to it. Without the patient's full cooperativeness, the therapeutic results are delayed, distorted, limited, or even prevented. (In *Collected Papers, Vol. 1*, p. 212)

Admittedly, this approach will demand from the therapist a high degree of integrity, creativity, and continuing willingness to expand personal horizons in the interest of professional competence. In order to enable the chronic client to become cooperative and responsive, the client must be given the immediate experience of the therapist's acceptance of the client's "needs as a human personality."

In the case of most chronic clients, words alone will not adequately communicate the therapist's acceptance. Generally, it will be necessary for the therapist to join the client, either on a metaphorical or literal level, in doing what the client is already doing. This will serve to undeniably communicate acceptance and appreciation.

While this is a demanding task, there are fortunately many strategies and techniques available to the therapist.

The best techniques and strategies will fail even the most competent therapist, however, if the therapist does not genuinely feel a sense of goodwill, acceptance, and appreciation towards the client. A crucial requirement for success is the therapist's integrity.

2

The Nature of
Ericksonian Utilization

Too many psychotherapists take you out to dinner and then tell you what to order. I take a patient out to a psychotherapeutic dinner and I say, ''You give your order.'' The patient makes his own selection of the food he wants. He is not hindered by my instructions which would only obstruct and confuse his inner processes. (Erickson & Rossi, 1973)

The utilization of the client's presenting behavior as an integral part of therapy (Erickson, 1955, 1965) and the utilization approach to trance induction (Erickson, 1958, 1959) are among Erickson's most important contributions to the field of hypnosis and psychotherapy (Erickson, Rossi, & Rossi, 1976).

The utilization techniques described in the following pages will frequently lead to the development of hypnotic trances. The specific focus of this book, however, is on utilization of the client's existing behavior, perceptions and resources to elicit therapeutic change. A comprehensive account of Erickson's utilization approach to hypnotic trance induction is beyond the scope of any single volume.

Utilization is the process of incorporating aspects of the client's current behavior and perceptions, current and past relationships, life experiences, innate and learned skills, and abilities into the therapeutic change process.

Both as a way of looking at the client and as a way of interacting with the client, Ericksonian utilization is a perspective of optimism and confidence in the client's ability to respond to treatment. The concept of utilization implies that every part of the client's behavior, personality, relationships, personal beliefs and situation is potentially valuable and useful in enabling the client to achieve more rewarding choices.

The concept of utilization is an essentially nonjudgmental way of looking at human behavior. Gilligan (personal communication, 1982) relates an anecdote in which Erickson says, "You cannot rigidly assign human values to human behavior. They're always changing."

It is crucial that the therapist maintain a nonjudgmental attitude if he or she is to succeed in enabling the client to become unstuck from rigid symptomatic patterns of behaving and perceiving. Direct or implied criticism of the client's behavior and perceptions are criticisms of the client's model of the world. Such criticism will serve only to strengthen the "resistance" patterns of an already chronically resistant client. If directly challenging a psychotic's belief system were a successful intervention strategy, it would have worked long before the client became a chronic client with a three-year or longer treatment history and no symptomatic relief. Erickson, (with Zeig) writes:

Concerning psychotherapy, most therapists overlook a basic consideration. Man is characterized not only by mobility but by cognition and emotion. No two people have the same ideas whether they are psychotically based or culturally based. When you understand how man really defends his intellectual ideas and how emotional he gets about it, you should realize that the first thing in psychotherapy is not to try to compel him to change his ideation; rather you should go along with it, and change it in a gradual fashion and create situations wherein he himself willingly changes his thinking (Erickson & Zeig, 1980, p. 335)

Particularly when working with chronic clients, it is crucial that the therapist be willing to meet the client where the client is currently at. Before any behavior or perception can be utilized (incorporated into the change process), three requirements must be met:

1) The therapist must accept and appreciate the problematic resistant behavior or perception as a legitimate piece of communication from the client regarding the client's current inner state and the client's model of the world.
2) The therapist must be willing to view the client's problematic resistant behavior or perception as a potentially valuable therapeutic resource.
3) The therapist must communicate this acceptance and appreciation to the client in an undeniable way.

Joining a chronic client in his symptomatic model of the world in order to therapeutically utilize the client's behavior and perceptions is an exacting and oftentimes a personally demanding task for the therapist. Since no two human beings are alike, each case requires a willingness to extend the therapist's personal limits in ways that may not yet be a part of the therapist's personal repertoire. However, to the extent that a therapist is unable or unwilling to do this, he or she will be handicapped in attempts to help the client.

It is crucial that the therapist's acceptance and appreciation of the client be real and not merely an attempt to "trick" the client into giving up his problematic resistant behavior or perception. Particularly in the case of the client who has been involved with the treatment system long enough to get labeled "chronic" or "schizophrenic," this very experienced client will be quick to sense any dishonesty on the part of the therapist. The therapist's attempt to utilize symptomatic behavior will then result in distrust and further loss of rapport. The therapist's integrity and respect for the client are crucial to the success of the Ericksonian utilization approach.

Chronic clients, more than any other client group, tend to demand a high degree of rapport, respect, and personal integrity from a therapist in order to respond. The world is too frightening a place for most chronic clients for them to be willing to take interpersonal risks with anyone they do not fully trust. As a result, the therapist must be scrupulously honest in all his interactions, or the client will respond by withdrawing further into the characteristic symptomatic behavior.

In the interest of accepting and appreciating a client's resistant behavior, it is useful to assume that behavior plays some functional role for the client. Symptomatic resistant behavior is frequently the client's attempt at self-protection from a world that is too overwhelming or frightening to face directly. Bizarre symptomatic behavior, such as catatonic withdrawal, violent movements, threats, and nonsensical statements, is often a defense against feared contact with other people.

Because of long-term experience with a given symptomatic mode of behaving, chronic clients tend to be, inadvertently, highly skilled at utilizing their therapists' reactions to the symptomatic behavior! In the back wards of a typically understaffed long-term, inpatient psychiatric unit, the chronic client remains chronic by using the therapist's reactions to the bizarre or otherwise symptomatic behavior as a way to push the therapist away and avoid contact. This serves to perpetuate the client's symptomatic behavior patterns.

This is not to imply that chronic clients consciously and strategically set out to avoid giving up their often painful and debilitating problematic perceptions and behaviors. Rather, chronic clients, being by their nature the world's most experienced clients, know on a practical intuitive level as much about utilization as any therapist. A chronic client will often put the therapist to the test to see how far the therapist is willing to extend himself to truly meet the client.

Accepting the client's symptomatic behavior or perception of the world, such as the psychotic's hallucination that she is walking in the midst of a group of angels, does not necessarily mean that the therapist has to personally agree that there are three dozen guardian angels standing in the room at the moment! In this and similar cases, acceptance implies merely that the therapist is willing to set aside all personal value judgments. The therapist is then able to accept the client's model of the world as a valid and accurate representation of that person's current experience. In this sense the therapist is able to honestly agree with the client and congruently express acceptance of all portions of the client's communication.

By accepting and thereby symbolically joining the client in his or her model of the world, the therapist enables the client to feel safe enough to make contact.

The symptomatic behavior that the client uses to remain a chronic or resistant client is also available for the therapist to use to successfully treat the client. Joining the client in his or her model of the world makes this achievable. Viewed in this manner, all symptomatic behavior is a potential resource for the therapist as well as the client.

The following excerpt will illustrate Erickson's use of the client's symptomatic behavior. Joining with the client in the symptomatic behavior, Erickson introduces a series of small changes that eventually result in the client voluntarily making a larger therapeutic change.

A patient in Worcester State Hospital in Massachusetts demanded he be locked in his room, and he spent his time anxiously and fearfully winding string around the bars of the windows in the room. He knew his enemies were going to come in and kill him, and the window was the only opening. The thick iron bars seemed to him to be too weak, so he reinforced them with string. I went into the room and helped him reinforce the iron bars with string. In doing so I discovered that there were cracks in the floor and suggested that those cracks ought to be stuffed with newspaper so that there was no possibility (of his enemies getting him), and then I discovered cracks around the door that should be stuffed with newspaper and I gradually got him to realize that the room was only one of a number of rooms on the ward, and to accept the attendants as a part of his defense against his enemies, and then the Board of Mental Health of the state of Massachusetts as part, and then the police system and then the governor. And then I spread it to adjoining states and finally I made the United States a part of his defense system; this enabled him to dispense with the locked door because he had so many other lines of defense. I didn't try to correct his psychotic idea that his enemies would kill him. I merely pointed out that he had an endless line of defenders. The result was: the patient was able to accept ground privileges and wander around the grounds safely. He ceased his frantic endeavors. He worked in the hospital shops and was much less of a problem. (Erickson & Zeig, 1980, p. 335)

THE HEART AND SOUL OF ERICKSONIAN UTILIZATION

At the heart of the Ericksonian utilization approach is a humorous, respectful and loving acceptance of the client's perceptions and behavior. A twinkle in the eye is a valuable if not crucial asset to the therapist who seeks to use this approach for successful therapy with chronic and resistant clients.

If the heart of the utilization approach is humor, respect, and acceptance, the soul is flexibility: "Anything the client uses to remain a client, the therapist can use to be a therapist" (Zeig, personal communication, 1984). There is little room in this approach for the therapist who requires the maintenance of a rigid authoritarian role with clients. As a colleague once said following the departure of an unsuccessful job applicant, "Our clients would eat that guy for breakfast!"

Flexibility, a secure willingness to extend oneself beyond regular boundaries, is likely to be required in order to succeed with chronic and resistant clients. If this were not so, the clients would not now be chronic clients or resistant clients at risk for becoming chronic clients.

RECOGNIZING AND APPRECIATING ALL THE
PERSONALITY ASPECTS

The attitude of appreciating all the interdependent aspects of each person is perhaps best conveyed metaphorically by a story told to the author by a young girl:

When I went away to college, I began to think about what it meant to be an adult. I thought about my mother and I thought about my father. They never had much money and they had had ten children, more or less one after the other. Living away from home I got used to the quiet of living alone, and I began to wonder how my parents had ever survived the strain of so many kids running around the house, sometimes being mischievous, occasionally hateful and ornery, and other times being sick and demanding care and attention at inconvenient times like late at night or on long car trips.

At Thanksgiving break I went home for the long weekend. I waited and waited and finally one night after the dishes were done, my mother and I were alone. I asked, "Mom, did you ever resent having all of these kids? Did you ever wish that maybe there weren't so many of us giving you all kinds of trouble all these years?" Mom sat looking at me with a sort of wondering expression on her face and a twinkle in her tired blue-grey eyes. She said, "Sure, sometimes I feel real tired at the end of the day and some days I sure would like to see these kids settle some quarrels without fighting, but really it's all right. Because that's the way people are, especially young people who are growing and changing every day . . . And besides, which one of you would you have me give up? Each one of you is necessary in order to make this family complete."

Therapists sometimes get the feeling that they need to get their clients to "give up" an apparently negative aspect of the client's personality "family." Even with best intentions on the part of both therapist and client, this endeavor is likely to fail. A far more fruitful approach is to appreciate and nurture the whole person, appreciating the beauty and worth of various personality aspects even when they're temporarily troublesome or mischievous like the children in the above story.

The utilization approach relies in part on the therapist's expression of an optimistic expectation of cooperation from the client. Towards this end, the therapist needs to develop a habit of looking at each client's idiosyncratic behavior with a mixture of acceptance, humor, hopefulness and respect. Traditionally, when a client fails to respond to therapy in ways that the therapist hoped, the client has been considered "resistant." This is a particularly unproductive way to view discrepancies between the client's behavior and the therapist's expectations!

All resistant behavior should be viewed for what it is, part and parcel of the total problem that the client brings to therapy (Erickson, 1965). Since the client's role is to get help with the problem and the therapist's role is to supply that help, all of the client's "resistant" behavior can be viewed by the therapist as evidence of the client's "unique" "way of cooperating" (De Shazer, personal communication, 1984).

Case Example
Utilization in Crisis Telephone Conversation with a Chronic and Resistant Client

The client was a 28-year-old man who had just lost his job and broken off an engagement. He had spent the last of his savings on her engagement ring which she refused to return. He lived alone. He had been repeatedly hospitalized for suicide gestures.

Client: I'm thinking of killing myself. I've even got a razor blade right here in my pocket.

Therapist: Sometimes talking about suicide is a cry for help. Do you think that you need to go to the hospital in order to get some support during this rough period?

Client: I've been to the hospital a bunch of times. I come back out and the feelings come up over and over again. I'm always spending all my money on other people, taking care of everyone else. They don't appreciate it. Going to the hospital isn't going to help.

Therapist: Okay, the *big* problem is obvious. You feel so terrible that you're thinking about killing yourself. What WE need to figure out is: What are the OTHER problems that make up this big problem? Let's list them.

Client: Well, I just broke up with my fiancée. I don't have a girl friend. I don't have a job. I don't have any money—none of my friends will lend me any. I asked my parents and my brother and they won't lend me any either . . . and right now I'm hungry.

Therapist: How hungry are you?

Client: Real hungry.

Therapist: Do you have any food in your house?

Client: Not much. My girl friend used to cook for me. I don't really know how.

Therapist: Would you be willing to go to the cupboard and the refrigerator and look?

Client: There isn't much there . . . but I'll go look.

Therapist: Okay, I'll wait while you do that.

Client: It's like I thought, just eggs, flour, and a can of peaches.

Therapist: Okay, we've got a problem, and that's what are you going to fix for yourself with flour, eggs, and peaches? It sounds like a menu choice of scrambled eggs, fried eggs, poached eggs, egg noodles, and maybe peaches on the side?

Client: I don't know how to fix these things.

Therapist: Do you know how to fix any of them?

Client: (*pauses for a long time, and then says, triumphantly*) Boiled eggs!

Therapist: That's one I didn't think of. Okay, now boil yourself a couple eggs and we can talk about some of these other problems and you can figure out those solutions, too.

Client: I feel really angry at Mary (fiancée). I took her out to dinner all those times and now she's moved out and she doesn't even offer to lend me any money or invite ME over for dinner. I was so good to her. I'm sick and tired of having people take advantage of me.

Therapist: How are those eggs?

Client: Nearly cooked . . . they actually look pretty damn good. . . .

Therapist: So now the eggs are nearly ready, what do you want to do about the *other* problems of the job and not having a girl friend?

Client: Well, I really don't care if I get a new girl friend right away, I'll get around to that. But about the job, I need to start looking . . . I'm going to sit here and eat my eggs, and then I'm going to go over to the laundromat across the street and pick up a used copy of this morning's paper. I'm going to make some calls . . . and tomorrow I'm going to start hitting the pavement looking. . . .

Therapist: This seems awful fast. Are you sure you feel ready to start looking and making these changes?

Client: Are you crazy? I've only got enough eggs to last maybe two days. Do you expect me to just eat eggs from now on?

Therapist: Good point. What are you going to do tonight?

Client: Watch T.V. Maybe I'll call a couple friends.
Therapist: They might know about a job possibility.
Client: They might. (*pause*) By the way, you don't have to worry. I'm not going to kill myself. But I might get pretty sick of eggs before I get a job. . . .
Therapist: Well you could always branch out and fix them in different ways.
Client: (*laughs*) I'll call you tomorrow and tell you how I'm doing.
Therapist: I'd like that.
Client: Me too . . . Bye.
Therapist: Good-bye.

In the above case, the client's immediate problem of being hungry served as a resource to focus his energy and sense of self-worth. Once he had solved the problem of what to fix for himself, this success could be used to substantiate the idea that he could and would resolve the other problems. He then spontaneously made sensible plans on his own. Problems often constitute resources when viewed in a flexible manner.

3

A Naturalistic Perspective for Hypnotic Trance

> It is the clinician's ability to evaluate and utilize patients' uniqueness together with the exigencies of their ever-changing real life situation that the most striking hypnotic and therapeutic results are most often achieved. (Erickson, Rossi, & Rossi, 1976, p. 20)

Erickson's utilization approach (Erickson, 1965) grew and developed in part from his recognition that all hypnotic trance phenomena occur naturally and spontaneously in everyday life situations.

Despite the absence of a formal hypnotic induction, the therapist's use of the utilization techniques discussed in this book will often lead to the development of a hypnotic trance in the client.

Since all hypnotic phenomena occur naturally and spontaneously in various aspects of everyday life, the use of "hypnosis" in therapy is not as black and white a distinction as it might initially appear. In choosing to discuss hypnosis with chronic and resistant clients, the author urges therapists to emphasize the naturalistic aspects of trance states, illustrating with examples from everyday life. This will give the client a secure, comfortable, and personally meaningful context to understand the experience.

NATURALISTIC EXAMPLES OF
SPONTANEOUS HYPNOTIC BEHAVIOR

Catalepsy

A woman is deeply engrossed in a telephone conversation. It is a hot summer day and her husband thoughtfully brings her a cool drink to sip while she is on the phone. Intent on the phone conversation, she does not notice him approaching. He places the drink in her hand, and her fingers automatically close around it. The woman's arm remains motionless, fixed in midair, holding the drink out in front of her for several minutes. She is preoccupied with the phone conversation and is unaware of her arm rigidly extended. A few minutes later, she reorients and becomes aware that her arm is still extended, holding the drink out in front of her. She takes a sip and sets it on a nearby table.

Another naturalistic example of catalepsy occurs with an avid sports fan who sits "frozen" in his or her chair while watching the deciding plays of the game. If the person is about to reach for something, such as a cold beer or pretzels, just as an exciting event occurs, he will "freeze" in midair and become motionless until there is some resolution in the game or a distraction occurs.

Children frequently evidence catalepsy, standing stiff and motionless with a hand raised and extended while waiting for an ice cream cone to be filled. There are numerous other similar examples of catalepsy in everyday life.

Amnesia

Introductions are made at a party and five minutes later one cannot remember the name of one of the people who was just introduced.

On a business trip, a man approaches a perfume counter to buy his wife a present. Although he has seen the bottle on the dresser a hundred times, he cannot recall the name of the perfume or even the bottle. He looks at all the bottles on the perfume counter. Occasionally accompanying him, his wife has bought her perfume at this same counter, so undoubtedly her brand is here, but he is unable to identify her perfume bottle among the others on display. He cannot even vaguely remember what it looks like! He decides to surprise her with some chocolates instead.

Hypermnesia

Carol is in love. She met him at a party 18 months ago and they have been dating ever since. When she thinks about that first meeting, even now she can remember every detail: the color of his eyes, the brand of cigar he was smoking, the cut of his shirt, the color of the sofa where they sat and talked, the music that was being played, the dress she wore, the scent of his cologne, and the line of poetry he recited to illustrate his point. Every time she hears that special song on the radio—the one that was playing that night— she recalls vividly every detail of that evening.

The old mailman knew every street, every house on every block in the neighborhood where he had worked for some 40 years. He knew the people who lived on those streets now, their names, and the names of all of their children, as well as the relatives who came to visit regularly and sometimes received mail there. He also remembered the faces and names of the people who had previously lived in those houses and had died or moved away years ago. He knew every dog by name and sometimes carried dog biscuits. He remembered which dogs became friendly after a gentle pat on the head and the possibility of a dog biscuit being offered. If asked, he could describe each house by its color as well as by its shape and number.

''My grandpa used to work for the railroad. His job was to write down the identification number of each car on a given train and then record the number of cars. He used to stand there along the track. He'd leave his pencil behind his ear and puff on his pipe while he watched those cars go by. When the last one went by, he'd walk into his office and write down the number of each car. Then he'd add up the number of cars and file the record. Sometimes his co-workers would write the numbers down to see if he made mistakes. He never did. He'd just puff away on his pipe and laugh.''

Age Regression

''My husband and I went to my daughter's kindergarten parent-teacher meeting. All the parents sat in those little chairs where the kids sat, facing that big green blackboard with the ABCs written across it and pictures of animals decorating all the bulletin boards. The teacher asked jokingly, 'How many of you can remember learning your ABCs?' She left the room for a minute, and pretty soon we were all laughing and fidgeting in our chairs, joking and feeling like we were back in kindergarten! My husband pulled my hair when the teacher wasn't looking. The woman in front of me was acting very playful and silly, not at all like she acts in meetings at the University Women's organization meetings. We were all acting like little kids. I guess it was those chairs and that ABC question . . . !''

The father got into the swimming pool with his brother and his young nephew. He playfully splashed the boy's father. Soon they were splashing and dunking each other the same way they had at camp 20 years ago, calling each other funny names and doing tricks in the pool. The boy was delighted.

''I bought a huge, very deep overstuffed couch, very modern. It actually resembles an enormous easy chair. My sister came over to visit and sat in it. She began to giggle and said, 'This chair is so big; I feel like I'm six years old.' She asked if I had any chocolate ice cream.''

Negative Hallucinations

''I knew those car keys were in the kitchen. I looked and looked and couldn't find them. Finally my roommate came in and saw them sitting right there on the shelf in full view. I must have looked at them a dozen times and not seen them.''

"I saw that handsome Jim Browne yesterday at the restaurant. I didn't notice whom he was sitting with."

"Mom, I swear I don't remember you telling me to take out the garbage. I didn't hear you tell me even once."

"It was only after he began to itch that he noticed that he had been sitting in a patch of poison ivy for the past hour. He hadn't seen it and couldn't remember hearing the camp counselor's warning that his wife described."

Positive Hallucinations

"I saw that big stick and I was SURE it was a snake. Scared the hell out of me."

"I can't believe we're out of coffee. I saw a full container in there this morning . . . and there's nothing there now."

"Honest, officer, I looked at my speedometer and it said 58. I *couldn't* have passed you at 66 miles an hour . . . "

"But Mom, I *heard* you say I could stay up until midnight!"

Analgesia and Anesthesia

An old lady is dying of rheumatoid arthritis. She has a great deal of pain despite her medication. Her days are spent in bed, broken only by her meals, medication, television and rare visitors. Her grandson is stationed in the army overseas. He writes to her faithfully and his letters bring a little bit of adventure into life. But her pain goes on and on. One day her grandson arrives unannounced, races into her room, and hugs her, obviously delighted to see her. She is shocked and overjoyed. Several hours later, recalling the incident, she realizes that while preoccupied with her grandson's presence, she had felt no pain. In fact, she had been unaware of any particular body sensations.

People sitting on a hard chair watching an entertaining movie will spontaneously develop analgesia and anesthesia. They will feel no discomfort from the chair, and will tend to be totally unaware of their body's discomfort. On the other hand, with a boring movie they will be aware of any slight discomfort.

Dissociation

A student is daydreaming during chemistry class. The teacher's words drone on and on. The student's mind is wandering off to a delightful memory of a scuba diving trip in the Caribbean. He remembers the vivid colors of the parrot fish, the graceful curves of stag horn coral. Abruptly the bell rings, jolting him away from his reverie. He has no idea of what was said in class, and has to arrange to get notes from a friend.

THE DEVELOPMENT OF A TRANCE STATE

A specific hypnotic trance state is more likely to develop if the therapist creates this expectation by telling the client that hypnosis will be employed as part of treatment (Zeig, personal communication, 1984). However, since trance is a naturalistic phenomenon, it is also possible for the client to develop a naturalistically absorbed and therapeutically responsive trance state without it being specifically defined as "hypnosis." Beahrs (1982) refers to naturally occurring hypnotic trance states as "spontaneous hypnosis."

Despite the absence of a formal hypnotic induction, the therapist's use of the utilization techniques discussed in this book will often lead to the development of a hypnotic trance in the client.

How to Recognize a Naturally Occurring Hypnotic Trance

Referred to by Erickson as "common, everyday trance behavior," this state is characterized by the client's absorbed attention, slowing of breathing, slowing of pulse, economy of body movement, flattening of facial musculature, absence of eye blinking, eye closure, catalepsy, alteration of time perception, alteration of voice tone and, most significantly, an increased therapeutic responsiveness (Erickson & Rossi, 1979, p. 16).

Erickson & Rossi (1979) describe these naturally occurring moments of trance:

> Even in ordinary conversation, one can take careful note of those momentary pauses when the other person is quietly looking off into the distance or staring at something as he or she apparently reflects inward. . . . Notice especially whether the person's eye blink slows down or stops altogether. Do the eyes actually close for a moment? Does the body not remain perfectly immobile— perhaps even with limbs apparently cataleptic, fixed in mid-gesture? (p. 16)

THERAPEUTIC ADVANTAGES OF THE TRANCE STATE

Increased Therapeutic Responsiveness

In treating chronic and resistant clients, the most useful of the trance phenomena described above is the client's increased therapeutic responsiveness. Described by Erickson & Rossi (1979) as "response attentiveness," this state is generally characterized by a slight change in facial coloration, a cessation of body movement, a fixed staring, and an absence of swallowing. Rossi describes clients in this state as having a similar "wide-eyed look of expectancy, staring fixedly into his eyes." He also refers to a "funny little smile (or giggle) of wistfulness or mild confusion" (p. 16).

Erickson cautioned the therapist not to "ruin these precious moments when the other is engaged in inner search and unconscious processes" (Erickson & Rossi, 1979). Instead, it is better for the therapist to remain quiet while the client further develops the "common, everyday trance" phenomena that result in feelings of comfort and relaxation and heightened therapeutic responsiveness. When allowed to fully develop, the client's state of heightened therapeutic responsiveness becomes the ideal opportunity to introduce a therapeutic suggestion or reframe.

The author has repeatedly observed clients in the above described therapeutic state of "response attentiveness" exhibiting a fixed, wide-eyed look characterized by dilated pupils, cessation of body movement, and a facial expression conveying complete trust and vulnerability. Clients in this state seem to also take on a somewhat childlike air.

How to Foster the Development of the Response Attentive State

The response attentive state will naturally begin to develop during certain moments in the therapy session; the client will evidence nonverbal expressions as described above. All that is really required of the therapist is to *not* interfere with the development of the response attentive state.

When the therapist notices, for example, the client staring fixedly, sitting motionless, with slightly dilated pupils, and an open, half-smile on his or her face, the therapist should stop talking! Whatever the therapist is saying is likely to be less important than the client's immediate internally focused exploration. The therapist should take advantage of this opportunity to pause for a few moments and enjoy firsthand discovery of the truth in Erickson's observation that people's faces are continually changing ''like sunsets.''

After a brief pause, the therapist can offer further support to the client by saying, as Erickson often did, ''That's right,'' ''Continue as you are,'' or a similar response. Eventually, the client will reorient and look expectantly at the therapist. This is the precise moment to introduce a therapeutic idea or a therapeutic reframe (Erickson & Rossi, 1979). The client's therapeutic response will be heightened. This is particularly valuable in working with chronic clients and resistant clients who are in danger of becoming the next generation of chronic clients.

Altered Time Perspective

Often the client will experience an altered sense of time as a result of a trance experience. This is no less true of a naturally occurring or ''spontaneous'' trance than in the case of a trance that has been formally induced by the therapist.

To the client, for example, an hour may subjectively feel like 15 minutes, or 15 minutes may perhaps feel like an hour or longer. This phenomenon is particularly useful when working with ''resistant'' clients who feel ''there is never enough time to adequately express and discuss feelings,'' or, conversely, with the client who feels restless and has a short attention span.

Hypnotic trance allows a plasticity in the client's time perception, enabling the client's individual subjective needs to be met. The author has repeatedly observed clients spontaneously altering their time perception in the service of their idiosyncratic therapeutic needs. If the therapist employs techniques that allow the client to develop the trance state, the client will tend to spontaneously develop an appropriate therapeutic alteration of time perception. This appears to occur regardless of whether or not the author defines the therapeutic relationship explicitly in terms of hypnosis.

Case Example

A very nervous, compulsive man arranged to be seen by the author for therapy every two weeks. He stated tensely, ''I am a businessman, I know I need to get over my problem and learn to relax and enjoy my life, but I don't have time to waste a single moment. I am just too busy to come in weekly; I doubt if I possibly can stay for the whole hour—I have places to go, people to see. I'll pay for the whole hour anyway, or of course more if I use it, but I want to warn you, I just can't stay sitting in one place for very long.''

Consistently, this client would develop, after only a few moments of casual conversation, a fixed, absorbed stare, and a wistful, half-smiling expression on his face. The author would simply remain quiet at this point, and after a moment, say quietly, ''That's right, why not really explore that for a minute?''

After another minute or two, the client would reorient and look expectantly at the author, who would then again introduce the primary issue of the therapy. The context of the therapy had now been altered for the client because of the momentary trance experience. The client would actively participate in the session. Characteristically, a few minutes after the end of the scheduled hour, he would exclaim, ''I can't believe it's five o'clock! I got so relaxed

. . . I can't believe I didn't notice the time!'' He then would leave, laughing. Eventually, this client's ability to therapeutically alter time generalized to his personal life where he discovered that he was capable of taking time to enjoy a full baseball game, smell a bouquet of flowers, fly kites and play with children. His business profits did not go down and he began to enjoy his personal life.

This client's astonishment about his altered time perception was made particularly humorous by the fact that the author's office contains a large antique clock. The clock has a large and very audible brass pendulum that continuously marks out the seconds and minutes in precise rhythmic order. This client always insisted on sitting facing the clock, so he could ''keep track of the time.'' Eventually he reported that at home and in other situations, he could become deeply relaxed simply by remembering the rhythmic ticking of the clock. Given a chance, clients will spontaneously respond to their own idiosyncratic therapeutic resources.

Diminished Resistance

Generally, it is in the client's conscious mind that ''resistance'' seems to reside. In a trance state, the client is likely to be more receptive to therapeutic assistance provided that it is truly in the client's best interest and in harmony with the client's individual personality needs. Usually, the deeper the level of the client's trance state, the more directly the therapist can speak without eliciting resistance.

An immediate advantage of hypnosis with a resistant client is that the hypnotic experience by its nature suggests a comfortable letting go, a shifting of internal perceptions. Since ''resistance'' is characterized by rigidity, a relaxed trance state is the antithesis of this.

Once a relaxed, comfortable trance state has been achieved, it remains as an available resource throughout subsequent sessions. Since a trance state developed in the therapy setting is usually a novel experience for the chronic or resistant client, it serves as a subtle yet powerful introduction to the notion that change and new learnings are possible.

A THERAPEUTIC PRECAUTION

Since the techniques in this book will frequently lead to the development of a trance state in the client, it is important to provide the client with a comfortable and easy way of reorienting at the end of the therapy session. This will avoid many difficulties.

A simple and reliable method is to routinely tell the client at the beginning of the therapy session:

> Before you leave here today I'm going to ask you to take a nice deep breath and then I'm going to say the words, "Okay (client's name)." When that happens, you will become increasingly alert and aware of your surroundings, returning to your everyday state of awareness with new learnings about yourself and a feeling of refreshment and relaxation.

The above prehypnotic suggestion is really a safety valve. Most clients who develop trance states in response to indirect hypnotic techniques will spontaneously reorient before the end of the session in response to alterations in the therapist's tonality, breathing and speech rhythm. However, since each client has an individual sense of timing, it is important to arrange a quick and effective way for the therapist to enable the client to reorient in a manner that fits into the constraints of scheduled appointments. The author routinely allows 90 minutes for each session, occasionally using less or more time according to the needs of the client.

The importance of the therapist conveying an attitude of comfort and security in the context of trance cannot be overemphasized. With many chronic clients, previous natural experiences of altered states may have included frightening episodes of psychosis characterized by severe depression, catatonia, hallucinations, anxiety and disorientation.

It should also be remembered that clients in a trance state tend to respond to communication in a very literal manner. Care should be taken to avoid using words that have contra-therapeutic double meanings. There is a story of a therapist who used hypnosis in creative growth groups. She used the word "yeasting" to describe one of the states in the creative process. Before the therapist became aware of the suggestive connotations of the word, several women in her group spontaneously developed yeast infections. It is important to carefully consider word meanings and associations when speaking to clients in a hypnotic state.

One way for the therapist to effectively deal with the difficulty regarding inadvertently using words with negative connotations or negative double meanings is to address this directly with the client at the onset of therapy. The author routinely tells clients:

> Now sometimes, despite my being very careful, I may occasionally slip and say the wrong word when I actually intended something else. Fortunately, we can trust that your unconscious mind will in every case automatically alter that word to a most positive and beneficial meaning that fits all of your needs in a healthy and meaningful way.

HYPNOSIS WITH PSYCHOTIC CLIENTS

In many ways, the behavior of psychotic clients can be said to resemble hypnotic phenomena. For example, dissociation, catalepsy (catatonia), confusion, and age regression are characteristics that can occur in the behavior of both trance subjects and psychotic clients.

Beahrs suggests that some psychotic clients may actually be evidencing "spontaneous hypnosis." He cites an example of a psychotic client who appeared to be in a state of spontaneous hypnotic age regression. He spoke to the psychotic client as if he had been the hypnotist who suggested an age regression and then proceeded in the manner of a good hypnotist in rapport with a regressed hypnotic subject. The client accepted Beahrs' suggestion that "her hypnotic skill was indeed a skill that she could use when needed under her full voluntary control." Within 20 minutes the client was no longer psychotic (Beahrs, 1982, p. 138).

The author has had similar experiences with psychotic clients who appear to be exhibiting trancelike behavior, and has in some cases achieved success in enabling psychotic clients to reorient within minutes or hours by using indirect hypnotic techniques of metaphor and associational cues. These techniques will be discussed in subsequent chapters in reference to psychotic symptoms of dissociation, confusion, and catatonia.

Over the past eight years, the author has experimented with direct and indirect hypnotic techniques in attempting to reduce the terror and confusion of psychotic clients and assist them in reorienting to a more comfortable, lucid state. As might well be expected, results have varied from client to client.

Generally, however, hypnotic techniques appear to be more helpful with those psychotic clients who are able to enter into a relationship with the therapist and others around him or her despite the psychotic behavior and perceptions. Success in reducing the psychotic's discomfort and enabling the client to reorient to a more lucid state through the use of hypnosis has been in direct proportion to the author's ability to develop a deep level of trust and rapport with the client. The author believes that psychotic clients are in a trancelike state that is apparently not in service of the "ego" (Beahrs, 1982).

It would appear that the client has gotten into the psychotic state out of inner desperation. Therefore, it is presumably necessary to provide the client with a strong context of safety and undeniable acceptance in order to enable the client to feel safe enough to reorient to an everyday, externally focused, lucid state.

The techniques included in this book have proven successful in accomplishing the above with *some* psychotic clients. However, the author has also seen a number of psychotic clients who require chemotherapy in order to regain the lucid state. While it is important that the therapist provide as many kinds of benevolent opportunities as possible to enable the psychotic to reorient, hypnotic techniques should not be misrepresented as a "cure-all" for psychosis.

The difference between psychotic, trancelike behavior and "common, everyday trance" behavior would appear to be the factors of whether the behavior is adaptive for the client, and whether the client retains an accurate reality-testing ability that enables him or her to reorient and function appropriately in the real world. In some cases, it will be possible for the therapist to create for the client a bridge from the psychotic trance to the more adaptive "common everyday trance" that results in new learnings and an increased ability to function productively.

4

Bypassing Conscious Blocks Through Interspersals and Presuppositions

If direct therapeutic suggestions were going to work for chronic and resistant clients, it would have happened long before they came to be considered chronic or resistant. The good-intentioned advice of family and friends, previous therapists, and teachers would have resulted in positive changes that resolved the client's problems!

The therapist's goal is to avoid getting caught up in arguing with the client about what is good for him or her. Such arguments tend to lead to more arguments. Instead, the object is to get the client out of therapy and actively and productively involved in living his or her life.

Therapeutic suggestions that are recognized overtly as such are easy for the "resistant" client to categorically resist. A chronic client is a resistant client "cum laude," having had years of experience in *not* responding to therapeutic suggestions.

In order to get a habitually nonresponsive client to respond, the therapist needs to structure the therapeutic messages in such a way that they are not easily recognized as such by the client on a conscious level. This frees the client to respond unconsciously in therapeutic ways that powerfully affect behavior and perceptions.

MULTILEVEL COMMUNICATION

Essentially, presuppositions and interspersals are forms of multi-level (Erickson, Rossi, & Rossi, 1976) communication. A multilevel task assignment is more likely to be accepted than the separate communication of the same two tasks. Erickson (1966) cites the following example:

> . . . A mother might say, "Johnny, as you put away your bicycle, just step over and close the garage door." (in *Collected Papers, Vol. II*, p. 262)

As Erickson points out, the above has the sound of a single task message characterized by two related details. This has the effect of making the actual two tasks sound easier. Furthermore, the combination of the two tasks in the single sentence makes refusing to do them more complicated. It is difficult for Johnny to clearly communicate whether a refusal would entail refusing to put away the bicycle, refusing to close the door, or both.

In the face of the above sort of complexity, it becomes far more simple for Johnny to say "yes" than to say "no" and enter into the confusion of linguistic ambiguity. The same is true for clients. This principle can be utilized in requests for two or more new responses, and in requests in which the new task "hitchhikes" on one of the client's characteristic behaviors.

Combining New Tasks into a Single Message

Several requests for new behavior can be combined, making the resulting suggestion difficult to refuse. For example, a woman who is a chronic overeater seeks assistance in changing her pattern. She has seen a number of therapists without success in changing her weight or her very negative self-image. She hates dieting, but does enjoy writing in her diary. She can be given the following multilevel task:

Therapist: As you are taking some time to jot down some of your feelings about the changes you are making this week in your eating habits, take a minute or two to identify a characteristic that you can appreciate about yourself.

In the above communication, three separate tasks are combined to resemble different aspects of one task. If the client were to say "no," it is unclear what the refusal would entail. Would "no" mean "I won't jot things down?" Would it mean "I refuse to notice changes in my eating habits?" Does it mean "I refuse to identify a characteristic that I can appreciate about myself?"

Saying "no" to the above task might also mean that the client is refusing all three or a selection of two of the three tasks. Clarifying what "no" entails would result in a great deal of verbal work for the client, making it far easier for the client to agree to do the requested multilevel task.

Other Examples

A very fearful client reacted with extreme terror at the idea of moving to a new apartment when her old apartment was scheduled to be torn down. She felt immobilized and unable to begin preparations for her move. She loved chocolate bars. She was given the following multilevel task.

> Go out and pick up three deluxe candy bars and then bring them home where you will eat one before you even think about beginning to pack your belongings, eating another one when the packing is half-done and a third one when you're all finished.

The packing got done, and she moved with the help of family and friends.

A very moody young man had a habit of striking pay telephones, doors and brick walls whenever he felt "out of control" in his anger. He had broken bones in his hands on several occasions and had also gotten into legal trouble for damaging private property. He was given the following directive:

> Go out and buy three large watermelons which you will keep in the back seat of your car at all times, destroying them with

your bare hands whenever you are angry and replacing them afterwards.

While he did not refuse the directive, the young man apparently took so much pride in the appearance and cleanliness of his car that he preferred controlling his anger to the mess he would cause with the "destroyed" watermelons.

Combining a Request for New Behavior with Inevitable Behavior

The same weight control client could also be given a therapeutic directive that combines a request for new behavior with a statement about the client's inevitable characteristic behavior:

Therapist: As you get out of your car to walk into your house tomorrow afternoon, pause for a minute and realize something new about your plans for dinner.

The client will inevitably get out of the car and will inevitably begin walking to the house. Since the suggestion to "realize something new" has been connected to the two other behaviors, it is difficult for the client to refuse without refusing to do something that she cannot help doing anyway!

Other Examples

A severely depressed client who refused to bathe or get out of bed was given the following message:

Lying there resting between those comfortable sheets after your bath, you may or may not find yourself wondering at what moment you began to feel increasingly comfortable.

One given characteristic is that this client will lie between those sheets. Eventually the client will find himself resting. Presumably, the client would like to feel "comfortable" and "increasingly comfortable." "After your bath" has now become inextricably linked to the other experiences in a way that is difficult for the client to resist. The client got up and took a bath!

A characteristically anxious client described his habit of walking around the park each evening. While the walk had no apparent effect on reducing his anxiety (sweaty palms, labored breathing, and a nameless fear), it was something that he "always" did after work, no matter what the weather was. He was given the following message:

> I don't know if it will be just before the walk, at the beginning of the walk, the middle, nearing the completion, or somewhat after that walk that you will experience an unfamiliar and perhaps initially surprising sense of well-being.

The client reported an "unfamiliar feeling of peacefulness" during his walk. Later on, the memory of the walk became a therapeutic resource for the client.

PRESUPPOSITIONS

A presupposition is an idea inserted into a sentence in such a way that the listener is obliged to accept the reality of that idea in order to make sense of the rest of the sentence. For example:

> When you get out of the hospital, Joe, do you think you will prefer to cook at home or eat out on weeknights?

In order for Joe to make sense of the question, he has to accept the presupposition that he will be eventually released from the hospital.

An interspersal is an idea that is sandwiched between other ideas and concepts in a sentence. This can be accomplished in a variety of of ways. For example:

> Last week, I said to my friend, Gina (client's name), "It's time to slow down and smell the flowers."

Since the therapist is merely quoting what she told a friend, the message cannot be directly understood as a message to Gina. This enables the therapist's message to travel past Gina's conscious resistance to be understood and received on a deeper therapeutic level.

Some Formulas for Presuppositions

The following words are of particular use in formulating presuppositions:

"When"
"While"
"After"
"Following"
"The day (week, month, year, 10 years, etc.) after"
"At the same time"
"What will (is, will be, etc . . .)"
"I wonder . . . "
"You can wonder . . . "
"I don't know when"
"I don't know which . . . "
"I don't know whether"

Here are some examples.

When.

When you have already accomplished your therapy goal there will undoubtedly be some interesting new goals for you to enjoy also.

(The use of "when" in this sentence implies that the goal will be accomplished and that the change will entail an experience of enjoyment.)

While.

While you go about your everyday chores and activities, pay attention to the subtle changes in your behavior.

("While" implies that the "subtle changes in . . . behavior" will occur while the client performs "everyday chores and activities.")

After.

After you begin to feel that nice calmness inside you, wait for the bell to ring and then enjoy taking that exam.

("After" implies that the feelings of calm will occur before the bell rings and before it is time to take the exam.)

Following.

Following the job interview, just go out for a nice lunch.

("Following" implies that the job interview will occur—that the client will, in fact, show up for it despite anxiety or any other problems.)

The day (week, month, year, 10 years, etc.) after.

The day after you start feeling better, you will notice some changes taking place.

("The day after" implies that the client will indeed start feeling better.)

At the same time.

At the same time you are getting ready for bed, subtle sensations of relaxation will begin to occur outside your awareness.

("At the same time" implies that the sensations of relaxation will occur as inevitably as the fact that the client will get ready for bed.)

What are you likely to feel when you discover that you have . . . ?

What are you likely to feel when you discover that you have made that change?

(The implication is that the change will occur.)

You can wonder what (significant person) is likely to think when they learn that you have. . . .

You can wonder what your family is likely to think (say) when they learn that you have made that change.

(The change will occur.)

What might a stranger notice about you after you have . . . ?

What might a stranger notice about you after you have made that change?

(Again, the implication is that the therapeutic change will occur.)

I wonder.

I wonder which of the two changes will occur first.

(The changes will occur.)

I wonder how you will know that the change will occur.

(The change will occur.)

I don't know when.

I don't know when this week you will stop smoking. It might be on Friday, it may be on Tuesday or Thursday . . .

I don't know if Y or Z will happen first.

I don't know if your conscious mind will know about the change first or perhaps your unconscious mind will be the first one to know . . .

(The change will occur.)

INTERSPERSALS

Milton Erickson once described his interspersal approach, along with nonrepetition, as the most important of his contributions to the practice of suggestion (Erickson, 1966; Erickson, Rossi, & Rossi, 1976).

Interspersals can take the form of embedded commands or messages designed to therapeutically alter the client's perceptions. Generally, interspersals are most effective if they contain a reference to a subject of general interest to the client.

The subject matter that interests the client will fixate the client's conscious attention, allowing the interspersed idea to be received on an unconscious level (Erickson, 1966).

For instance, in speaking to a gardener, Erickson embedded some therapeutic messages for comfort and pain relief in the following way:

> And soon the tomato plant will have a bud form somewhere, on one branch or another, but it makes no difference because all the branches, the whole tomato plant, will soon have those nice little buds. I wonder if the tomato plant can, JOE, FEEL A KIND OF COMFORT. You know, Joe, a plant is a wonderful thing, and IT'S SO NICE, SO PLEASING just to be able to think about a plant as if it were a man. Would such a plant HAVE NICE FEELINGS, A SENSE OF COMFORT as the tiny little tomatoes begin to form. . . . (Erickson, 1966)

EMBEDDED COMMANDS

When Erickson intersperses, ''JOE, FEEL A KIND OF COMFORT,'' he has delivered an embedded command (Bandler & Grinder, 1975).

Embedded commands are therapeutic directives that are interspersed within other more general communication to the client. Embedded commands can be inserted in stories about tomato plants and other subjects geared to the client's idiosyncratic interests and preferences, or they can be inserted in everyday conversations through inflections and the use of quotes.

In order to increase effectiveness, the embedded message is emphasized indirectly through the therapist's alteration of tone, rate of speech or body language.

Some Effective Ways to Strengthen Embedded Commands

A common mistake the author has observed is for therapists to RAISE their speaking volume to emphasize the embedded command. It is far more subtle, and consequently more effective, for the therapist to emphasize the embedded command by lowering the speaking volume. Similarly, a slightly downward speech inflection is likely to be more effective than an upward inflection.

Therapeutic messages can also be indirectly emphasized for the client by the therapist making subtle shifts in posture or flexing an arm or leg while delivering the message. In group situations, the therapist can indirectly emphasize the embedded command by turning to look at another client while pointing folded hands or a partially extended finger at the intended client recipient! Surprisingly, clients rarely appear to consciously notice this incongruence in the therapist's communication!

Testing the Effectiveness of Delivery Style

One way that the therapist can test personal effectiveness in delivering embedded commands and therapeutic messages is to embed some observable directives and watch for the client's response. For example:

Reading a new novel last night, I thought to myself, SARAH (client's name), it's a nice experience to stop reading novels for awhile and then discover that you can BE THIRSTY for a new story. I read for an hour, decided to GET UP AND GET A DRINK OF WATER and then read for another hour.

If the above embedded commands have been given appropriate emphasis, the client will become thirsty and be likely to get up and get a drink of water during or shortly after the session.

Here is another example:

There are a lot of little idiosyncratic habits people have that no one really thinks seriously about. For example, how often in a movie theater do you see someone and know from their behavior that they are obviously acting on an urge to SCRATCH YOUR NOSE. Now this is an everyday sensation that most people experience at least once a day. Some people initially ignore the urge, some people actually consciously fight it, but sooner or later people ENJOY THE PLEASURE OF GIVING INTO THE URGE TO SCRATCH YOUR NOSE.

If the above embedded messages are delivered with sufficient indirectness and emphasis, the client is likely to spontaneously scratch his or her nose. Similar harmless "tests" can be employed in the therapy context to make sure that the therapist's messages are reaching the client.

Case Example
Use of Presuppositions and Interspersal

The client was a 42-year-old woman who came to the author because she felt "hopeless" and "unable to go on" in the face of her recent divorce. She had been married for 11 years and had been in therapy for the past five years with a long list of therapists she described as having failed to help her. She described her problem as "feeling hopeless, apathetic, empty," but could not be more specific. Repeatedly she used the phrase, "at the end of my rope."

The client's situation was complicated by financial problems. While trained both as a cosmetologist and as a real estate agent, the client felt unable to work or to make a decision about future vocational directions. When asked why, she would slump in her chair and repeat that she was "at the end of my rope." The author's repeated attempts to acquire further information were unsuccessful.

The author believes it is crucial for a client's problems to be defined in solvable terms, and therefore diagnosed the client as suffering from "loneliness, boredom, and unemployment." The client concurred, but solemnly and firmly stated, ''I can't change, and there isn't a damn thing you or I can do about it.'' She spoke these words with tears in her eyes.

The therapist's direct attempts to challenge the above belief served only to elicit from the client more tears and increasingly vehement affirmations of the truth of her previous statement.

As a young therapist, the author might have decided from the above statement that the client was not a suitable candidate for therapy. However, her presence and request for additional appointments, coupled with her obvious unhappiness, implied a motivation that contradicted the message, ''I can't change.''

Unless an intervention could be achieved, this resistant client, after five years of unsuccessful therapy, was clearly on her way to becoming a long-term chronic client. The client's past history indicated that direct therapy techniques would probably not be successful.

The author met with the client for eight consecutive months. During this time, the client continued to be vague and evasive about her feelings about the divorce, her reasons for feeling unable to change, and the details of her feelings about her self. She did, however, willingly and spontaneously engage in ''small talk'' about how she was spending her days, the soap operas she was watching, her plans for the weekend, and her armchair observations of the current real estate market. In response, the author discussed recipes, speculated about the current television soap operas, wondered aloud about the real estate job market, and listened with apparent sympathy to the client's regular complaints about being ''unable to change,'' and ''at the end of my rope.''

Therapeutic messages, presuppositions, and embedded commands were regularly interspersed in the ''small talk.'' After one month, the client began to invite acquaintances over for dinner. After two months, she began to inquire about possible jobs. After three months she began to apply for jobs. The fifth month she appeared to hit a slump and did little socially or vocationally. The sixth month, she became more energetic, continued to entertain women friends, began to play golf, and got a job. The seventh month she began to date, and the eighth month, she left therapy with the complaint that she was now ''too busy.'' (!)

During the course of therapy, the author made repeated attempts both directly and indirectly, to elicit more specific and current information about the client's current feelings and ongoing difficulties. These attempts were consistently fruitless; however, the client continued to request therapy appointments!

On the other hand, the client did not appear willing to do the therapy work on her own, with the support of the therapist. She categorically and consistently refused to do any therapeutic homework assignments. However, when the author questioned her about whether it was worthwhile for her to continue in therapy, the client would angrily point out that "I still have my problems, don't I?" Furthermore, in all good conscience, the author could not think of anyone she disliked sufficiently to justify the referral of this client! So the client stayed in therapy.

The "therapy" consisted of a series of weekly, then every other week, and eventually monthly, "small talk" conversations between therapist and client in which therapeutic messages, embedded commands, and presuppositions were interspersed with sympathetic responses and trivial exchanges:

Therapist: How are you doing today?
Client: Terrible, I don't want to talk about it.
Therapist: Any particular reasons you don't want to talk about it?
Client: I just don't.
Therapist: What would you rather talk about?
Client: (*ignoring therapist's direct question but responding indirectly*) Rachel on "Another World" is getting married again, and Bert is still in love with her but she's in love with this other guy.
Therapist: What do you think will happen? I mean that story has been going on for years. Sometimes I don't see it for months and then I find myself WONDERING . . . WHAT'S REALLY HAPPENING INSIDE the minds of all those characters? And I TUNE IN AND LEARN SOMETHING NEW . . . Maybe A NEW FEELING going on in one of the characters, maybe someone has fallen in love, or a new character has come into the picture. With all that drama going on there, right on the old T.V., there's NO REASON TO SIT AROUND BORED. I

don't know how they ever managed in the past without those
soap operas.

Client: I know, I have it on all day, do my housework with it on,
take naps with it on. And I can't stand to miss an episode. I
lay half-awake all night wondering what happened. . . .

Therapist: Well, of course you wonder, 'cause sometimes IT'S HARD
TO PREDICT THE EXACT CHANGE that is going to happen
next in those shows even though, from one week to the next,
those CHANGES HAVE ALREADY BEGUN to take place. . . .
Well, tell me this, what is Rachel going to wear to her wedding,
and is this her third marriage now?

Client: Her third or fourth I guess. It's no big deal on those shows
to get divorced.

Therapist: Yeah, they kind of imply that DIVORCE DOESN'T HAVE
TO BE THE END of the world. One thing I can't help hoping
is that Rachel can BEGIN TO FIND SOME PEACE after all
those things she's been through. After five years, I'm kind of
attached to that character.

Client: Me, too. I hardly know what to do on Saturdays and Sun-
days. I hate all those sports shows on T.V. I'm having my sister
and her son over for dinner next Friday night. I'm making
them my mother's meatloaf recipe and scalloped potatoes. It's
so much work to cook for people. I don't cook for myself . . .
it's too much work. I'm really at the end of my rope with this
divorce. . . .

Therapist: It is a rough time for you.

Client: It's terrible.

Therapist: I can see how it is. . . .

Client: (*changing subject*) I saw in the paper today about this new
stain remover that will get anything out, ink, blood, lipstick,
almost anything and you can use it on any fabric.

Therapist: That sounds great.

Client: Yeah, I told my sister about it and she said she'll look at her
supermarket—it's bigger than the one I go to—and she's going
to try to pick me up some.

Therapist: Yeah, it's SO NICE . . . with all the false advertising and
all those new products on the market all the time . . . to FIND

SOMETHING NEW THAT REALLY WORKS. Sure you have to spend a little money but IT'S WORTH THE RISK to be able to LOOK FORWARD TO SOME SATISFACTION. . . .

Client: I have this wine stain on a linen tablecloth I have tried everything on. . . .

Therapist: Even bleach?

Client: Even bleach.

Therapist: I have a friend, who knows how to, SARAH, REALLY FIX THOSE PROBLEM stains, but she has to USE A LOT OF DIFFERENT THINGS. I think she gets a lot of stuff from *Heloise's Hints*, you know that book?

Client: Yeah, I got a copy for free once with something else. . . .

Therapist: Well, anything she has in that book, you can FEEL COM-FORTABLE about using, and if you put her recommended stuff on a stain, you know it's going to GO TO WORK on that stain and the same solution is going to WORK JUST FINE WHETH-ER IT'S TODAY, TOMORROW OR MONTHS FROM NOW. . . . She just really knows what she's doing. . . . My mother and my grandmother swear by her. We all have copies of her paperback book.

Client: Me, too.

In the above example, subjects of interest to the client were employed by the therapist to fixate the client's conscious attention. Interspersed therapeutic messages, embedded commands, and pre-suppositions could then be received by the client on an unconscious level. Similar interspersal techniques can be employed with any subject matter that is of particular interest to a client.

5

"Yes" Sets and "No" Sets

The rapport is the means by which the therapist and patient secure each other's attention. Both develop a "yes" set or acceptance of each other. (Erickson & Rossi, 1979, p. 2)

Establishing an acceptance set or a "yes" set (Erickson, 1975; Erickson & Rossi, 1979; Erickson, Rossi, & Rossi, 1976) is a key ingredient of success with otherwise "resistant" clients.

Developing a "yes" set with a client transforms resistance into a productive, and frequently strikingly beautiful experience of the "I/thou" nature. The author has repeatedly experienced the above "yes set" phenomenon with a wide variety of resistant clients formerly regarded as "chronic, unmotivated, recalcitrant" and occasionally tagged with even worse labels by therapists at lunch and after-work "winding-down" sessions.

A "yes" set is a state of mind characterized by agreement and deep acceptance. In successful therapy, this sort of acceptance is a two-way street in which both therapist and client develop a simultaneous "yes" response to each other (Erickson, Rossi, & Rossi, 1976). Two simple and classical components used by Erickson to develop a "yes" set were truisms and compound suggestions.

TRUISMS

Erickson used truisms (Erickson, Rossi, & Rossi, 1976, 1980) in two different ways. One way was to refer to simple already established facts such as a person's name, gender, current address, etc. In the following excerpt Erickson uses this sort of truism to develop a "yes" set.

> *E*: Now I'm going to ask you, is your first name Ruth? [Ruth nods yes.] That's right. Are you a woman?
> *Ruth*: Yes.
> *E*: You just nod your head or shake your head in answer. Are you a woman? [Ruth nods yes.] Are you sitting down? [Ruth nods yes.] (Erickson & Rossi, 1981, p. 87)

Another, more subtle way that Erickson employed truisms to create a "yes" set was by "recognizing and acknowledging current experience" (Erickson & Rossi, 1981, p. 87). By asking Ruth in the above excerpt if she is sitting down, Erickson begins to utilize current experience to further develop the client's "yes" set.

Prerequisites for Developing a "Yes" Set

Before beginning to employ the truisms, however, the therapist should take a moment to establish his or her own sense of deep comfort and security. A favorite relaxation method should be employed between therapy sessions to ensure that the therapist not only maintains healthy good feelings, but embodies these feelings of relaxation and healthy self-appreciation which will be implicitly conveyed to the client.

The therapist then needs to adopt an attitude of deep appreciation for both the self and the other (client). Most therapists, by virtue of having chosen therapy as their profession have an appreciative and compassionate view of their clients. This attitude of appreciation, acceptance and compassion on the part of the therapist towards the self and the client is prerequisite to developing a "yes" set in the client. As a former client of the author (a kid who had lived in ghettos and survived a year on the roughest streets of New

Orleans) once said, "You can't just talk the talk—you have to walk the walk."

There is always something to appreciate about a client, and the appreciation can begin with any detail about the client and then spread to the WHOLE client.

"A Good Tooth"

The author once overheard a gruff, obviously seasoned therapist respond to a troubled novice at a family therapy convention. The new therapist was complaining that there were some clients whom she found totally unlikeable and with whom she felt unable to focus on any positive details. The mature therapist made the following response:

> There's always something to love about every client. Sure it's sometimes hard to find right away . . . but there's always SOME-THING and then the feeling can grow into an acceptance and appreciation of the whole person. . . .
> . . . Like this guy I saw a week ago. . . . He was unwashed, unkempt, hostile, he smelled bad . . . and I thought, "There's got to be SOMETHING." I sat there looking at him and after a few seconds I noticed that he had only one tooth in his mouth. Only one, but at least he had one tooth. I thought, "This guy has ONE GOOD TOOTH and I can at least appreciate THAT." And then the feelings of appreciation began to spread to the rest of the guy. I found myself wondering about the kind of life he must have had that caused him to become this way, the tragedies and high points of his life, his loves and griefs . . . and pretty soon I felt all the appreciation I needed to feel, with some extra to spare. It's always there if you just let yourself really connect with the person. . . ."

In using truisms to develop a "yes" set, the therapist needs to simply employ "truths" about the client that are either currently self-evident or known to be true. This can be achieved in a nat-uralistic, conversational manner. At worst, repeatedly employing truisms with an otherwise resistant client may result in the client becoming bored, thereby making it easier for him or her to get on with therapy to escape the tedious flow of benign and friendly truisms!

For example, a therapist might begin a session by verifying the following truths about the client:

Therapist: Your name is Harry. (*Client nods yes.*)

Therapist: We've spoken on the phone, but this is the first time you've come to my office. (*Client nods yes.*)

Therapist: You told me on the phone that you've felt frustrated by your previous experiences in therapy.

Client: (*nodding yes*) That's right.

Therapist: And now it's two o'clock on Tuesday afternoon and you're here and I'm here. . . .

(*Client nods, visibly relaxes, and adjusts body in chair into more comfortable position.*)

Therapist: And you're sitting in that tan chair and I'm in this brown chair, the clock is ticking, and outside some birds are singing . . . (*commenting on shared ongoing experience*).

(*Client begins to look somewhat impatient, begins to play with a paper clip he picks up from the adjoining table. He looks at the therapist with an expression of expectancy and curiosity.*)

Therapist: And I'm wondering if you'd be willing to tell me just exactly how you would like things to be for you in your life after completing this therapy together. . . .

Client: The changes I'd like to see happen are. . . .

Generally the more frightened, skeptical, cautious, angry, or unmotivated the client appears, the more truisms will be required to fully develop the "yes" set. Once the set is fully developed, the client will be able to bring an attitude of acceptance to the therapeutic endeavor.

When one is using truisms with a client to develop a "yes" set, the client's nonverbal communication provides the indication of when to drop the truisms and reap the benefits of the now established mutual "yes" set. After nodding, or saying yes to several truisms, generally the client will begin to look a little bored. She will have adjusted to an apparently comfortable sitting position and will begin to look at the therapist in an increasingly expectant, curious manner. This is the time for the therapist to begin the work at hand.

COMPOUND SUGGESTIONS

Once a "yes" set has been established, a compound suggestion can be introduced. Essentially, a compound suggestion consists of two statements. The first is a truism, connected by a slight pause or an "and," and then followed by a therapeutic suggestion (Erickson, Rossi, & Rossi, 1976, 1981).

The first part of the sentence continues the acceptance or "yes" set. The therapeutic suggestion contained in the second half of the sentence then "hitchhikes" along on the acceptance created by the truism. There are three forms of compound suggestions that the author has found to be particularly useful in working with chronic and resistant clients.

In its simplest form, the compound suggestion is a truism based on the client's perceptions or behavior which is followed by the therapeutic suggestion. For example:

> You're sitting here looking at your watch . . . (*truism*) and (*or pause*) . . . you really do have time to begin to RELAX FULLY FOR THE NEXT FEW MINUTES . . . (*therapeutic suggestion*)

or

> You are here today even though you would rather be at the beach or out with your friends . . . (*truism based on client's description of feelings about coming to therapy today*) and (*or pause*) YOU WILL LEARN SOME VALUABLE THINGS ABOUT YOURSELF as a result of coming today (*therapeutic suggestion*).

A second, more subtle kind of compound suggestion is for the therapist to connect the therapeutic message to a truism about the therapist's rather than the client's behavior (Erickson, Rossi, & Rossi,

1976; Erickson & Rossi, 1981). Since the therapist has control over his or her own behavior, by simply doing the behavior he or she reinforces the therapeutic suggestion. For example:

> I'm going to talk to you . . . (*truism*) and . . . you can CONSIDER YOUR FEELINGS IN A NEW WAY about that important decision (*therapeutic suggestion*)

or, a more subtle version

> You can NOW CONSIDER YOUR FEELINGS IN A NEW WAY about that important decision . . . (*therapeutic suggestion*) and . . . I'm going to talk to you (*truism*).

Since the therapist has control over her own behavior, by merely continuing to talk, the therapist reinforces the suggestion to "consider your feelings in a new way."

A third form of compound suggestion employs a truism involving surprise, followed by a "clarifying message" designed to help the client establish some emotional equilibrium, and then the actual therapeutic directive (Erickson, Rossi, & Rossi, 1976, 1981). The surprise may take the form of humor or a psychological shock. For example:

> You can discover that you have some time on your hands when you look down and notice that you're wearing a watch . . . (*humorous pun contained in truism*) and . . . you really do have the ability to enjoy using that time well . . . (*clarification*) (*pause*) . . . so why not take a few minutes to LET GO AND DEEPLY RELAX (*therapeutic suggestion*).

The humor contained in the bad pun in the first statement has the effect of "depotentiating the clients' habitual conscious set" (Erickson, Rossi, & Rossi, 1976; Erickson & Rossi, 1981) so that the client is receptive to further "clarification" to counteract the shock. The "clarification" supplied actually gives the client a reminder of his inner resources, leaving the client receptive to the third statement, which is the therapeutic suggestion.

Erickson & Rossi (1980b) gave the following example given for a compound suggestion employing shock [bracketed notes added by author]:

> Secret feelings you have never told anyone about . . . [shock contained in truism] can be reviewed calmly within the privacy of your own mind [clarification containing therapeutic suggestion] for help with your current problem [therapeutic suggestion].

The words, "secret feelings," tend to create a psychological shock that makes the client extremely receptive to resolving the shock with the two indirect therapeutic suggestions that follow (Erickson, Rossi, & Rossi, 1976, 1981).

The emotional shock can be created by any emotionally significant words or ideas. The clarification and therapeutic suggestions are then used to resolve the shock.

Here are some other examples:

> When someone you love has just died . . . (*shock*) you begin to remember as well as the other feelings the memories of all the good times you had together . . . (*clarification*) and those good times can give you help in finding strength to take positive risks in various new relationships (*therapeutic suggestion*).

> A disappointment can be very painful even if no one knows about it but you . . . so taking the time to reap the harvest of the learning that resulted is your right and your reward . . . supplying needed help with the problem you carried here today.

> Not having a date one Saturday night . . . eventually leads to the ability to enjoy being alone with yourself now . . . providing the luxury of individual tailored truths to apply to the needs you have today.

"NO" SETS: UTILIZING NEGATIVITY

A "no" set is essentially the opposite of a "yes" set. Everything the therapist asks or suggests is met by the client with an all-encompassing "no." Everything is seen by the client in the worst possible light, and disagreement is a repetitive and reliable pattern.

In the case of a client with a very well-developed "no" set, the therapist can actually repeat back to the client what the client had just said, and the client will still find a way to disagree! For example:

Client: My name is Susan and I'm here for my two o'clock appointment with you.
Therapist: Please come in.
Client: I'd rather not. I don't really want to be here. My probation officer sent me.
Therapist: Your probation officer sent you.
Client: Well . . . not exactly. She told me I'd get in trouble if I didn't come, so I decided to come even though I don't want to be here.
Therapist: You don't want to be here.
Client: It's not that, I'd just rather be somewhere else.
Therapist: I wonder where you'd rather be.
Client: (*sounding miserable*) I can't think of anywhere. I'm too depressed about having to be here by court order when I don't want to be here.
Therapist: You said your name is Susan, right?
Client: Well, actually, my friends call me Suzy.
Therapist: What would you like me to call you.
Client: That's up to you. I'm not going to tell you what to call me.

How to Change a "No" Set to a "Yes" Set

When a client presents a "no" set, the therapist can develop a therapeutic "yes" set using the client's pattern of negation.

The therapist responds to the client with statements comprised of a truism based on the client's communication followed by a negation in the second half of the sentence. The sentence is then ended with a questioning tone. Following is an example of this truism + negation + questioning tone.

Client: It was very inconvenient for me to come here today, and I'm not feeling very hopeful about coming to therapy.

Therapist: You have had some past experiences that cause you to feel not very hopeful about therapy, and yet despite the inconvenience, you had the courtesy to drive here and keep this appointment anyway, DIDN'T you?
Client: Yes, I did.

The above pattern of truism + negation + questioning tone will make it necessary for the client to say "yes" in order to continue to maintain the negative position. For example:

(Yes) I am feeling not very hopeful.

(Yes) it was inconvenient.

(Yes) I kept the appointment.

Conversely, if the client continues to say "no," he will be expressing a positive feeling. Either way, an acceptance set will be developing and a positive tone will be set for the therapy. For example:

No (I am now feeling hopeful).
No (it was actually convenient).

A third negation, "No, (I did not keep the appointment)," is ruled out by the client's physical presence.

Case Example

Client: I've been waiting to see you for the past ten minutes. Your secretary said you just finished your last appointment. My name is Robert. . . .
Therapist: Please come in. . . .
Client: I'd rather not. I don't really want to be here. My social worker sent me.
Therapist: (*smiling*) You'd rather NOT be here. . . .
Client: That's right . . . I really don't want to be here.

Therapist: There are a lot of places you'd rather be and things you'd
    rather be doing, are there NOT?
Client: Yeah . . .
Therapist: And you'd probably disagree if someone told you that
    this was going to be helpful, is that NOT right?
Client: Yeah—right (*lips beginning to twitch*).
Therapist: So it seems like this is a situation that's NOT very pleas-
    ant. . . .
Client: Yes, it's not . . . (*smiles ironically*).

The Conspiratorial Tone

At this point in working with a client who presents an initial "no"
set, it is often useful for the therapist to shift his or her physical
position to a slightly more intimate one such as leaning forward
slightly in the chair or moving slightly closer to the client. The
therapist then should look the client in the eye and speak in a soft,
conspiratorial tone:

Therapist: So . . . since you DON'T want to be here, which by the
    way is understandable under the circumstances . . . and there
    are a lot of things you'd rather be doing . . . why NOT see
    if we can find a way to get you out of this situation of need-
    ing to come in for therapy as fast as possible . . . (*conspiratorial
    tone*).
Client: (*entering the office*)Where do you want me to sit?
Therapist: Anywhere you like. . . .
Client: Did they tell you about my case . . . ?
Therapist: Only a little . . . what you say is more important to
    me. . . .
Client: Well, it started about two years ago just after my father
    died . . . (*conspiratorial tone*).

The therapist's assumed role of co-conspirator will tend to create
a bridge of acceptance between client and therapist, enabling the
client to respond in a similarly confiding manner. The "no" set has
now become a fully developed "yes" set.

In summary, the necessary therapeutic communication pattern for transforming a "no" set to a "yes" set consists of the following basic components:

truism + negation + question (repeated several times)
followed by
therapist's shift to a more intimate posture + conspiratorial tone

When one is employing this technique with very experienced resistant clients, it is likely that the first part of the sequence will have to be repeated several times (pacing) before the client will follow the therapist's communication (lead) to a co-conspiratory, "I/thou" communication mode.

In some cases, it may take weeks or months before the client builds sufficient trust to respond therapeutically. Generally, however, the client will have developed a "yes set" after four or more "yes" set responses to questions containing negatives.

If the client reverts to the "no" set or otherwise does not respond to the therapist's conspiratorial tone and postural shift, it is an indication that the therapist has not yet adequately reflected the client's point of view in developing the "yes" set.

The therapist in this situation simply needs to return the focus to understanding and accurately reflecting the client's point of view (truism), then following with a question in the form of a negative question.

Even after a "yes" set has been established with a client, it is often useful to occasionally intersperse a question containing a negation between other communications to the client. This will tend to ensure that the "yes" set continues. The following case example illustrates the process of transforming a "no" set to a fully developed "yes" set.

Case Example

Carol was a 38-year-old woman who was in the process of pursuing a divorce from her abusive and alcoholic husband. The separation process had continued for several years, and the client had nearly become a ''professional'' client, seeking the help of a long series of therapists over the past seven years.

Client: It doesn't seem like anyone can help me . . . it all seems hopeless.

Therapist: What is it that you would most like help with?

Client: I really don't know, it feels like everything is going wrong in my life right now.

Therapist: Can you give me some examples?

Client: Well I don't know where to start.

Therapist: There's a lot that you feel is going wrong right now (*truism*) and you DON'T (*negation*) know where to begin to describe it.

Client: (*sighs*) Yeah. . . .

Therapist: And you seem to be feeling pretty weary (*truism*) and I'm wondering where we can start that won't (*negation*) be as difficult as previously.

Client: I don't mind it being difficult if it works in the long run. I'm just tired of the way things are going and have been going.

Therapist: You're tired of the way things are, and maybe you're even somewhat worried that things could actually get worse (*conveys acceptance and possible exaggeration of client's negative frame*), are you NOT (*negation*)?

Client: (*nods*) That's right.

Therapist: And now we're sitting here together (*truism*), and it's less than five minutes into this session (*truism*) isn't it (*negation*)?

Client: (*looking puzzled*) That's right—yes.

Therapist: And you're in your thirties still (*truism*), is that not right?

Client: Yes.

Therapist: And you've been suffering through this divorce and other problems for a long time now, haven't you?

Client: Yes. . . . It's been over three years, and it really hurts (*tears come into her eyes*).

Therapist: And you would like to be able to realistically look forward to some happy times in the future, would you not?

Client: (*breathes deeply and momentarily relaxes body posture*) I sure would.

Therapist: You've been hurting for a long time now . . . (*client nods*) you're tired of the pain . . . (*client nods*) you're still only in your thirties . . . (*client nods*) and you would like to be able to enjoy your life more . . . (*client nods*) which is the purpose of being here today . . . (*client nods*) . . . so why not begin by letting yourself start to think about how you would be feeling and spending your time at the end of successful therapy?

Client: (*closes eyes for a few seconds before beginning to speak*) Well, I wouldn't be thinking about Jed all the time . . . I'd have a job that I liked, a more comfortable place to live, and I wouldn't be overweight like I am right now. And I . . . hopefully, would have some new friends, maybe I'd be dating someone.

Therapist: When you think of that, how does it make you feel?

Client: Pretty good . . . except for the losing weight part. That seems pretty near hopeless. The more I feel bad, the more I eat, and then I feel bad because I'm fat and there it goes again . . . (*shrugs, throws hands in the air and lets them fall on her lap in an energetic and exaggerated fashion*).

Therapist: So it would be a pretty amazing experience for you to actually lose the extra weight as well as resolve the other problems too, wouldn't it?

Client: (*smiles*) It sure would!

Therapist: Well, why not (*interspersed negation*) start by telling me a little about how you've been spending your time and how you've been feeling this past week.

Client: Okay. Well, Monday I saw my attorney. The divorce date is final a week from next Tuesday. Ever since then I've been pretty much just sitting around my apartment doing nothing. I suppose I should feel happy that it's almost over. I truly want the divorce. But I just feel this horrible sadness, like ''what kind of life is this I'm living?'' I'm not dating anyone, I hate my job, I've spent the last three years fighting with my ex-husband over legal details. I don't seem to know where I'm going any more and . . . I want to find out. I WANT TO TAKE CHARGE OF MY LIFE.

At this point, the ''yes'' set has been established and the client is ready and able to earnestly begin the therapeutic endeavor. It should be noted that the client's body movements became more active and energetic once the "yes" set was fully established.

For example, even though the client was talking about her hopelessness about losing weight, she began to communicate in a far more energetic and expressive fashion in the context of the "yes" set. She threw her hands up in the air, and began talking in longer, far more descriptive sentences.

While the form of expression will vary from client to client, generally, a change to a more expressive and active communication style is often an indication that the "yes" set has been fully established. The therapeutic endeavor will now be much less difficult for both client and therapist.

6

Strategies for Communicating Acceptance in an Undeniable Way

CASE EXAMPLE FROM MILTON ERICKSON (1965)

George had been a patient in a mental hospital for five years. He was simply a stranger who, around the age of 25, had been picked up by the police for irrational behavior and committed to the state mental hospital. During those five years, he had said, "My name is George," "Good morning," and "Good night," but these were his only rational utterances. Otherwise, he uttered a continuous word salad, completely meaningless as far as could be determined. It was made up of sounds, syllables, words, and incomplete phrases.

For the first three years he sat on a bench at the front door of the ward and eagerly leaped up and poured forth his word salad most urgently to everyone who entered the ward. Otherwise, he merely sat quietly, mumbling to himself. Innumerable efforts had been made by psychiatrists, psychologists, social service workers, other personnel, and even fellow patients to secure intelligible remarks from him, all in vain. George talked only one way, the word salad way. After approximately three years he continued to greet persons who entered the ward with an outburst of meaningless words, but in between times he would stay silently on the bench, appearing mildly depressed, but somewhat angrily uttering a few minutes of word salad when approached and questioned.

Erickson joined the hospital staff in the sixth year of George's stay. He obtained all available information about George's ward behavior and learned also that patients or ward personnel could sit on the bench beside him without eliciting his word salad so long as they did not speak to him. With this total information, a therapeutic plan was devised. A secretary recorded in shorthand the word salads with which he so urgently greeted those who entered the ward. Those transcribed recordings were studied, but no meaning could be discovered. Then these word salads were carefully paraphrased, using words that were least likely to be found in George's productions, and an extensive study was made of these until Erickson could improvise a word salad similar in pattern to George's but utilizing a different vocabulary.

Then all entrances to the ward were made through a side door some distance down the corridor from George. Erickson began the practice of sitting silently on the bench beside George daily for increasing lengths of time until the span of an hour was reached. Then, at the next sitting, addressing the empty air, Erickson identified himself verbally. George made no response.

The next day the identification was addressed directly to George. He spat out an angry stretch of word salad to which Erickson replied, in tones of courtesy and responsiveness, with an equal amount of his own carefully contrived word salad. George appeared puzzled and responded with another contribution with an inquiring intonation. As if replying, Erickson verbalized still more word salad.

After five or six interchanges, George lapsed into silence and Erickson promptly went about other matters.

The next morning appropriate greetings were exchanged with both employing proper names. Then George launched into a long word salad to which Erickson courteously replied in kind. There followed brief interchanges of word salad until George fell silent and Erickson left for other duties.

This continued for some days. Then George, after returning the morning greeting, made meaningless utterances for four hours. It taxed Erickson greatly to make a full reply in kind, while missing lunch. George listened attentively and made a two-hour reply, to which a weary two-hour response was made. (It was noted that George watched the clock throughout the day.)

The next morning, George returned the usual greeting properly but added about two sentences of nonsense. The author replied with a similar length of nonsense. George replied, ''Talk sense, Doctor.'' ''Certainly, I'll be glad to. What is your last name?'' ''O'Donavan, and it's about time somebody who knows how to talk asked. Over five years in this lousy joint . . . '' (to which was added a sentence or two of word salad. The author replied, ''I'm glad to get your name, George. Five years is too long a time . . . '' (and about two sentences of word salad were added.)

The rest of the account is as might be expected. A complete history sprinkled with bits of word salad was obtained by inquiries judiciously salted with word salad. His clinical course—never completely free of word salad, which was eventually reduced to occasional unintelligible mumbles—was excellent. Within a year he had left the hospital, was gainfully employed, and returned to the hospital at increasingly longer intervals only to report his continued and improving adjustment. Nevertheless, he invariably initiated his report or terminated it with a bit of word salad, always expecting the same from Erickson. Yet he could, as he frequently did on these visits, comment wryly, ''Nothing like a little nonsense in life, is there, Doctor?'' to which he obviously expected and received a sensible expression of agreement plus a brief utterance of nonsense.

After he had been out of the hospital continuously for three years of fully satisfactory adjustment, contact was lost with him except for a cheerful postcard from another city. This gave a brief but satisfactory summary of his adjustments in a distant city. It was signed properly, but following his name was a jumble of syllables. There was no return address. He was ending the relationship on his terms of adequate understanding.

During the course of his psychotherapy, he was found hypnotizable, developing a medium trance in about 15 minutes. However, his trance behavior was entirely comparable to his waking behavior and repeated tests showed no therapeutic advantages. Every therapeutic interview was characterized by judicious use of word salad.

The above case (*Collected Papers, Vol. 1*, pp. 213–215) represents a rather extreme example of meeting a patient at the level of his decidedly serious problem. Erickson was at first rather sharply criticized by others, but when it became apparent that inexplicable imperative needs of the patient were being met, there was no further adverse comment.

THE IMPORTANCE OF COMMUNICATING ACCEPTANCE

In order to therapeutically utilize behavior or perceptions, the therapist must first succeed in communicating acceptance and appreciation to the client in an undeniable way. The fact that therapeutic empathy and rapport are necessary conditions for effective therapy has been documented in the past (Berenson & Carkhuff, 1967). Developing rapport with a "resistant" client is the responsibility of the therapist. If the client already had that skill, he wouldn't have the need to resist!

Symbolic Verbal and Nonverbal Communication

Chronic clients present a particular challenge because they often demand an exquisite degree of rapport in order to respond. A technique sometimes described as "pacing" is a particularly powerful technique available to the therapist attempting to achieve rapport for the purpose of doing effective therapy with chronic and resistant clients. "Pacing," "leading," and "anchoring" are techniques identified as a part of a system of psychotherapy/communications termed Neurolinguistic Programming (Bandler & Grinder, 1975, 1979; Grinder, Delozier, & Bandler, 1977; Dilts, Grinder, Bandler, Delozier, & Cameron-Bandler, 1979).

The origins of pacing, leading, and anchoring lie in Bandler and Grinder's observation of Milton H. Erickson. The author terms these techniques examples of symbolic verbal communication and symbolic nonverbal communication, a form of implicit communication.

This chapter will discuss and illustrate various uses of precise verbal and nonverbal symbolic communication techniques for the purpose of communicating acceptance and appreciation in an undeniable way and enabling the client to follow the therapist's lead to voluntarily choose new and rewarding behavioral and perceptual alternatives.

PACING

Specifically, pacing is the technique in which the therapist selects a portion of the client's ongoing communication and simultaneously feeds it back to the client. In its essence, pacing is a naturalistic behavior that occurs spontaneously in two or more people who are in a state of deep rapport. For example, people who are in deep harmony tend to spontaneously "mirror" each other's behavior. Everyday naturalistic examples of this phenomenon include a mother opening up her own mouth as she spoon-feeds her baby, two lovers adopting a similar posture as they sit talking on a park bench or eating at a restaurant, musicians moving in precise rhythm with each other, close friends accurately finishing each other's sentences. The two lovers will lean toward one another in similar postures; their movements will tend to be synchronized. The musicians will tend to continue to move their hands and feet in synchrony even for a few minutes after a song has ended; their body postures will be similar, breathing patterns often identical while playing the music. The baby will tend to open his mouth at the same time the mother does as she holds the spoon near the baby's lips. This occurs unconsciously. These experiences provide a sense of intimacy, harmony, security and trust between the participants that goes far beyond words.

Pacing can occur both verbally and nonverbally. As symbolic verbal communication, pacing occurs when communication both includes and exceeds the explicit meaning of the words being said. This occurs naturalistically when two people use the same sorts of words to describe their experiences. In therapy, this occurs when the therapist succeeds in "talking the client's language." Besides the explicit meaning of the words, the fact that the communicator is using words and topics favored by the listener constitutes a deeper, indirect "meta-message" of acceptance and appreciation. Since this deeper message is received indirectly, on an unconscious level, it tends to bypass conscious fears or other kinds of resistance, and stands a good chance of being an undeniably positive experience for the resistant client.

Speaking the Client's Language: Topical Pacing

Symbolic verbal communication can take several different forms. The therapist can speak the client's language by talking about topics that the client is likely to be interested in or has demonstrated some affinity for. On a deeper level, when the therapist talks about topics that are appealing or meaningful to the client, the therapist is communicating a message beyond the explicit meaning of the words, a message that, "We have some understanding in common. I am willing and able to meet you on your own terms regarding things that are meaningful and important in your life."

Erickson spoke the client's language topically by being able to talk about and use examples about mothering and child rearing when talking with mothers, discuss work with people who worked at specific trades, and communicate symbolically with virtually everyone by bringing up stories about learning experiences from childhood. Since every adult has been a child and has experienced learning, these stories implicitly constituted symbolic verbal communication in the client's own language.

Speaking the Client's Language: Verbal Pacing

Another form of symbolic nonverbal communication occurs when the therapist uses the same sort of descriptive words that the client tends to use. Termed "verbal pacing," this technique is based on the concept of *representational systems* (Bandler & Grinder, 1975; Dilts et al., 1979).

Representational systems are conscious modes of processing (taking in, storing and later recalling) sensory experience. As human beings, we make contact with the world, external and internal, through the five physical senses of sight, smell, taste, hearing, and touch. Bandler and Grinder (1975) propose three main ways that people organize sensory experience:

1) *Visually*—by creating internal images.
2) *Auditorily*—by listening to internal dialogue.
3) *Kinesthetically*—by having "feelings" about something.

Furthermore human beings tend to have a preferred representational system (Grinder, Delozier, & Bandler, 1977) that is more highly favored than others in regard to given experience. This will tend to vary from person to person as well as within the person.

For example, when the author reads a book and later on recalls that stored experience, the recollection is a visual image, similar to seeing a movie. On the other hand, when remembering how to play a piece of ragtime piano music, she tends to remember "feeling" how her fingers move across the keyboard to produce certain rhythms and sounds. The ragtime music memory is accessed for her in a kinesthetic representational system.

Someone else might remember how to play a piece of ragtime music by remembering the "sound" of the melody and syncopations. For that person, the ragtime piano playing memory is accessed through an auditory representation system. In the case of reading a novel, a highly auditory person might remember the "sound" of the "words" describing scenery and the dialogs between characters. A highly kinesthetic person may remember the "feelings" that different parts of the book evoked.

In terms of everyday communication, the language people use will tend to reflect their most highly favored representational system. Their choice of predicates (adverbs, adjectives, verbs) will tend to reflect their way of taking in, accessing and storing experiences (Dilts et al., 1979).

Verbal pacing is accomplished by first identifying the client's primary representational system by listening to the descriptive words (predicates) the client uses to communicate his ongoing experience. Then the therapist responds to the client using like predicates. In this way the therapist "speaks the client's language."

Identifying Primary Representational Systems

Essentially this is simply a matter of listening to the descriptive words (adjectives, nouns, and verbs) the client is using to describe the ongoing experience. Grinder, Delozier, & Bandler (1977) state that natural language is literal.

Comments such as "I see what you are saying" are often communicated by people who organize their world primarily with pictures. These are people whose most highly valued representational system is visual. They are literally making pictures out of what they hear.

Dilts et al. (1979) cite further examples of the use of predicates in natural language that reflect the speaker's representational system:

(a) *Visual*—I can SEE the pattern now. I just can't PICTURE myself doing that. I need a CLEARER IMAGE of the problem. I just go BLANK. That casts some LIGHT on the subject. LOOKING back on it now I can begin to SEE the light. An enlightening and COLORFUL example.

(b) *Auditory*—That SOUNDS about right. I can HEAR your unwillingness. Everything suddenly CLICKED. There's a lot of STATIC inside my head. I can really TUNE into them. ASK yourself if it's right and LISTEN carefully for the answer . . . .

(c) *Kinesthetic*—I FEEL like I'm still REACHING for an answer but I just can't seem to get a HANDLE on it. It's a HEAVY problem. I need to get in TOUCH with my blocks. He's got a SOLID understanding of what's involved . . . .

The therapist's rapport with the client will be enhanced to the degree that the therapist speaks the client's language, matching verbs, adjectives, and adverbs and topics of interest to those of the client.

Nonverbal Symbolic Communication

A client's experience can also be paced nonverbally. Bandler & Grinder (1975) identify three forms of nonverbal pacing: 1) full direct mirroring; 2) partial direct mirroring; 3) partial indirect mirroring. There are distinct advantages to each of these three forms of nonverbal symbolic communication.

Just as the first step in doing verbal pacing is listening to the client's words, the first step in doing nonverbal pacing involves paying attention to the client's nonverbal language. This involves observing the client's:

voice tone
voice rhythm
voice volume
body movements
body posture
other nonverbal behaviors

1) Full Direct Mirroring

One powerful way of conveying acceptance, or "getting in tune" with another person, is to simultaneously DO all of the above things that person is doing. This kind of pacing is called *full direct mirroring*. In its most extreme form, this is essentially mimicry, and risks making the other person feel "mocked" or self-conscious. On the other hand, in the case of an extremely withdrawn, dissociated, psychotic client, this extreme form of full direct mirroring may be necessary in order to effectively reach the client and establish trust and rapport.

In full direct mirroring the therapist literally mirrors the client. The therapist does exactly what the client does in terms of body posture, body movements, breathing rates, and all other nonverbal communication behaviors. The therapist's nonverbal behavior literally constitutes a mirror image of all of the client's nonverbal behavior.

There will be times when it is not desirable for the therapist to do all of the nonverbal behaviors the client is doing. Besides possibly making the client self-conscious, this may have the effect of disorienting the therapist or hampering his or her effectiveness. For example, if the therapist is pacing an agitated client and matches the client's shallow rapid breaths, the therapist is likely to experience some of the light-headedness that the client is feeling. It will then become increasingly difficult for the therapist to remain alert, centered and focused. Doing everything (the extreme form of direct mirroring) that the client is doing can also occasionally produce the effect of the therapist beginning to experience some of the actual feeling states the client is experiencing. In some cases, for the purposes of empathy, this may be useful. In other cases, this may hamper the therapist's effectiveness by producing a disoriented, anxious, defocused state in the therapist.

2) Partial Direct Mirroring

In cases where it is not desirable for the therapist to employ full direct mirroring, pacing may be accomplished through *partial direct mirroring*. This consists of matching *some* of the therapist's behavior to *some* of the client's behavior. For example, the therapist might swing her left leg in synchrony with the client's leg and simultaneously match the tone and volume of the client's voice. However, since the client is breathing rapidly and shallowly, and is sitting in a position that would cause the therapist physical discomfort, the therapist does not match those nonverbal behaviors. The therapist accomplishes partial direct mirroring in this case by only mirroring the client's leg swing and matching voice volume and tone.

3) Partial Indirect Mirroring

A third way of doing nonverbal pacing is to match some of the client's nonverbal behavior with a different but simultaneously synchronized behavior from the therapist. This is called *partial indirect mirroring* and constitutes a very effective form of symbolic nonverbal communciation.

In this technique, the therapist selects one or more portions of the client's ongoing nonverbal behavior and synchronizes a response in the form of a simultaneous but different sort of nonverbal behavior from the therapist. For example, the therapist could synchronize the tapping of his third finger to the client's breathing rate. Or the therapist could lower or raise her voice volume in synchrony with the client's eye-blink rate. The tone of the therapist's voice could be synchronized with the client's facial expression. (This is a common naturalistic example of how therapists spontaneously exhibit partial indirect mirroring with their clients.) Partial indirect mirroring occurs when the therapist feeds back some of the client's behavior in a different mode.

Pacing Chronic and Resistant Clients

Once a therapist succeeds in accurately pacing a client, resistant behaviors tend to no longer constitute a difficulty. If the therapist is willing to continue pacing the client, one of two things usually occurs:

1) The client, reassured (or perhaps intimidated?) by the level of rapport achieved through pacing, spontaneously drops the resistant behavior.
2) The therapist, by virtue of identifying closely enough with the client to accurately pace him, achieves enough understanding of the client's behavior to successfully accept and utilize the client's resistant behavior to lead to therapeutic change.

This is not to say that pacing "cures" the problem. Rather, pacing cures the client's resistance to the therapeutic intervention. For example, a shot of painkilling medication does not "cure" a broken leg; instead it makes that patient comfortable enough to allow the doctor close enough to set the leg in such a way that the patient's natural healing processes can operate. The patient will eventually walk again. Similarly, pacing allows the therapist to get close enough to the client to initiate a change process that ultimately draws on the client's own resources.

To the extent that a therapist is willing and able to accurately pace a resistant client, there is no such thing as a resistant client. In the case of chronic clients, extreme measures will more than likely be demanded from the therapist in order for the client to eventually respond by entering into rapport. This client is initially likely to "test" the therapist by trying to outlast him—a time-honored strategy of most chronic clients! However, if the therapist is willing and able to continue pacing the client during every contact, the client will generally respond by at least temporarily joining the therapist in a context of rapport. Therapeutic communication and intervention will then be possible.

A Summary of Pacing

Topical pacing—therapist matches topics discussed to client's areas of interest.

Verbal pacing—therapist matches predicates to client's primary representation system.

Nonverbal pacing—there are three types of nonverbal pacing:

1) *Full direct mirroring*—therapist matches *all* nonverbal behavior with client's nonverbal behavior.
2) *Partial direct mirroring*—same as #1 except therapist matches some (not all) of the client's nonverbal behavior.
3) *Partial indirect mirroring*—therapist matches some of the client's nonverbal behavior with therapist's different nonverbal behaviors.

PACING AND LEADING

Once the therapist has adequately paced the client, a deep level of trust and rapport will result; the client will be in a highly receptive state. At this point, by changing what he is doing, the therapist will be able to *lead* the client into new behavior. In order to do this effectively, the therapist must remain sensitive to the client's ongoing needs for acceptance and reassurance. Each lead should be followed by several instances of additional pacing behavior. This will ensure that rapport is maintained.

A delightful naturalistic example of pacing and leading may be found among New Orleans jazz musicians. Imagine a saxophone player who plays a melody in harmony with the other members of the band for several minutes (pacing). He then introduces a new melody (leading) which the other members of the band pick up. They all play the same melody for awhile, and then another musician in the band leads with a new melody. Pacing and leading can also be observed in the spontaneous movements of couples on a dance floor, among children at play, and in many other everyday situations.

When done accurately, pacing communicates a message of complete acceptance and appreciation in a powerful way that cannot be denied. Adequately pacing a client gives the client the opportunity to respond more comfortably and easily to the therapist's lead of therapeutic change.

Pacing and Leading with Chronic Clients

It is particularly important when working with chronic and resistant clients to intersperse leads with a far larger proportion of pacing. In addition, it is essential that the therapist lead the client by introducing small and gradual changes that are reasonable within current capabilities. In pacing and leading, effectiveness is contingent on the therapist's willingness to be sufficiently sensitive to the client's natural change rate and abilities to respond.

Chronic and resistant clients often require the more extreme forms of pacing. One of the reasons chronic clients have remained chronic is that they have a tendency to outlast their therapist's willingness to work towards obtaining rapport (pacing).

In the case example at the beginning of this chapter, Erickson successfully paces a chronically psychotic client, eventually leading him to less constricting, more "normal" behavior. In an extreme form of full direct mirroring and verbal pacing, Erickson initially spends time sitting with the client on a bench, and subsequently speaks the client's language to the extent of talking in a word salad. He then gradually leads the client into more normal intelligible speech and behavior, interspersing the lead with more word salad (pacing).

In this case example, Erickson initially paces the client by sitting silently next to him on the bench (nonverbal pacing). He repeats this several times. He then "leads" by introducing himself to the "empty air." (This also could be viewed as pacing the client's psychotic behavior.) The client does not immediately respond to this initial lead. Erickson leads again the following day, addressing the introduction directly toward George. George responds with angry word salad which Erickson paces with more word salad (verbal pacing); however, Erickson's tone of "courtesy and responsiveness" constitutes a simultaneous nonverbal lead. The client responds to this lead by altering the angry tone of his word salad to an inquiring tone. Erickson again paces with word salad.

The next day, Erickson leads with a greeting employing the client's full name. George follows this lead by addressing Erickson in kind and then lapsing into more word salad which Erickson continues to pace. This is followed by a subsequent session in which the client follows Erickson's lead of returning the morning greeting and then proceeds to talk in word salad for four hours. Erickson paces this fully by speaking in word salad for the next four hours. The client responds with two more hours of word salad which Erickson then paces for another two hours!

Erickson does not abandon the client or give up at this point as many therapists might be tempted to do after spending several hours with a chronically psychotic client speaking only in word salads. On this occasion Erickson devoted twelve hours to listening to and speaking in word salads! The therapist's willingness to extend himself is a crucial condition for successful therapeutic intervention with most chronic clients. In working with chronic clients, the author has frequently observed similar situations in which the client appears to "test" the therapist's willingness to stay involved. Often this is a turning point in the therapeutic relationship.

In the subsequent session, Erickson leads with an intelligible greeting to which the client responds with an intelligible greeting following by more word salad. At this point Erickson's pacing evokes an opposite, polarity response in the client: "Talk sense, Doctor." Throughout the remainder of treatment, Erickson continues to lead with appropriate normal language while pacing the client's decreasing word salad with additional word salad. As frequently occurs in the case of chronic clients, the symptom does not disappear entirely. Instead it takes on a far more manageable and less constricting form: The last contact Erickson has with this man is a postcard that includes a bit of word salad. Erickson's intervention succeeds in enabling this man to live independently in a far less restricted, more socially acceptable and presumably more rewarding lifestyle.

This case is, of course, an extreme example of pacing and leading. It is included here, however, because chronic and resistant clients frequently tend to require similar extreme measures in order to respond therapeutically.

Erickson states:

> Sometimes—in fact many more times than is realized—therapy can be firmly established on a sound basis only by the utilization of silly, absurd, irrational, and contradictory manifestations. One's professional dignity is not involved, but one's competence is. (Erickson, 1980, in *Collected Papers, Vol. I*, p. 213)

Before ending this discussion, the author wishes to call attention to the amount of meticulous preparation Erickson undertook in arranging this rather extreme intervention strategy. He first learned all he could about the client's history, and was aware of the previous intervention strategies employed by "psychiatrists, psychologists, and social service workers." In addition, Erickson arranged for a secretary to record the client's word salads, which were then studied for possible meanings and subsequently used to precisely formulate Erickson's own word salads. In this way, Erickson precisely and accurately spoke the client's own language, symbolically communicating acceptance and appreciation in a respectful and undeniable way.

Considerations for Employing Extreme Forms of Pacing with Chronic Clients

Despite Erickson's reference to initial "censorious" criticism from colleagues, the fact that this sort of intervention was tolerated by the staff of the hospital in which he worked implies that he had succeeded in conveying his therapeutic purpose to his colleagues. In attempting any sort of extreme pacing technique, the following conditions should first be met:

1) The therapist should spend adequate time getting to know the client's problem, his personality, social history, and treatment background.

2) The therapist should know what treatment outcome he wishes to enable the client to achieve.

3) The therapist should make it a point to reach understanding and agreement with colleagues and supervisors regarding the treatment goal and the strategies employed. The act of explaining and discussing an extreme and perhaps highly imaginative and creative strategy with colleagues and supervisors will often be helpful in enabling the therapist to further refine the goal and the strategies he decides to employ. Simply acting like a client (full direct mirroring) does not necessarily constitute therapy in and of itself!

7

Establishing New Therapeutic
Resources Through Associational Cues

I left the farm a long time ago, so did my kid sister. On the farm
we ate supper, and dinner was at noon . . . the evening meal
was supper. And we left the farm and lived in the cities ever since.
My sister made a couple trips around the world and dropped in
to see me. I hadn't seen her for a number of years. We were talking about the various sights she encountered traveling around
the world, all of a sudden my wife heard us say "supper." My
wife was born in Detroit and grew up there, and my sister and
I were referring to the evening meal as "supper." Long association on the farm had left its trace and meeting her evoked that
pattern. And you watch people, and I wonder what their patterns are going to be . . . don't have any preconceived idea. Look
for one little bit of evidence, and another bit of evidence, pretty
soon it adds up. You learn patterns by adding minimal bits of
information and by all observations. . . . '' (Gordon & Meyers-
Anderson, 1981, p. 120)

ASSOCIATIONAL CUES

An associational cue (Erickson, Rossi, & Rossi, 1976; Erickson &
Rossi, 1979, 1980b) is a stimulus that elicits an unconscious response.
The response can be external or internal in nature and may or may
not be within the person's conscious awareness.

74

Virtually every sensory experience (sight, sound, smell, touch and taste) functions as a potential associational cue for the experience at hand. These associational cues can be systematically developed and utilized for therapeutic purposes.

The experiences elicited by an associational cue may be a feeling, an automatic response such as a handshake elicited by the cue of an outstretched hand, an internal visual image such as a mental "picture" of a close friend or a childhood home, or an auditory response such as a memory of words or melody.

For example, handing a hungry person his favorite kind of cookie or sandwich may elicit an externally observable response of reaching for the food, putting it up to his mouth, and beginning to chew.

Internally, the cookie or sandwich may be eliciting certain associated feelings, remembered conversations, visual images, etc., connected to previous experiences with that particular object. In *Swann's Way* (1928), Marcel Proust described a powerful feeling of happiness evoked by a "madeleine" cookie and a cup of tea:

> No sooner had the warm liquid and the crumbs with it, touched my palate than a shudder ran through my whole body, and I stopped, intent upon the extraordinary changes that were taking place. An exquisite pleasure had invaded my senses . . . . (p. 54)

In some cases, a person may consciously recognize the relationship between the associational cue and the experience elicited. For example:

> This smell and taste reminds me of my Mom's kitchen when I was a little girl,

or

> that exact color reminds me of feelings about my childhood sweetheart who used to wear a dress that color,

or

> That music takes me back to my senior year in high school.

When people are feeling ill, they tend to respond favorably to childhood foods associated with feelings of comfort and security. Food that tastes and smells ''just like Mom used to make'' is often highly lauded. Frequently, eating a dish that does indeed taste ''just like Mom's'' or ''grandma's'' will function as a temporary age regression, recalling feelings, images, associations from an earlier time.

Similarly, listening to music that was popular during the time of one's youth or a couple's courtship often functions to elicit happy feelings.

Conversely, Vietnam veterans suffering from Post-Traumatic Stress Disorder sometimes evidence an unpleasant associational response to stimuli that remind them of events they experienced in combat. A client seen by the author responded with terror whenever he heard loud noises such as fireworks and sirens, and responded with panic whenever he saw someone attired in the khaki green color that he and his fellow soldiers had worn in combat.

Proust (1928) describes the conscious phenomenon of associational cues in vivid detail:

> And once I had recognized the taste of the crumb of madeleine soaked in her decoction of lime flowers which my aunt used to give me . . . immediately the old grey house upon the street where her room was, rose up like the scenery of a theater to attach itself to the little pavilion, opening on to the garden . . . . (p. 58)

In other cases, the effect of the associational cue may be outside the person's conscious awareness, and the feelings or behavioral response will be produced without the person consciously knowing how or why this occurs.

> An exquisite pleasure had invaded my senses, but individual, detached, with no suggestion of its origin . . . . Whence did it come? (Proust, 1928, p. 55)

FACTORS AFFECTING STRENGTH AND RELIABILITY OF ASSOCIATIONAL CUES

Associational cues are sometimes established the first time a given experience is connected to a sight, sound, feeling, touch, smell or taste. In other cases, the associational cue is formed only after several repetitions in which the cue is associated to the experience. For example, a woman who stops to buy donuts and coffee to take with her on the bus may after weeks and months come to associate the sight of a donut shop with the memory of bus rides.

In order for an associational cue to be formed after only one experience, the cue must either be very unique or the experience characterized by intense emotions. Examples of this sort of cue include, but are not limited to, the following:

Sights

A small boy is unprepared for his mother's sudden death. He has never seen yellow roses before. After this single experience he continues to associate yellow roses with the feelings of sadness and shock that accompanied his mother's death. Twenty years later, the associational cue of yellow roses is still potent in evoking these feelings. He may be consciously aware of the connection, or in other cases be confused when a dinner guest's gift of a bouquet of yellow silk roses evokes disturbing feelings.

A woman carries a bouquet containing lilies of the valley on her wedding day. Several years later, she and her husband are shopping for a house to purchase. One of the houses they are shown contains a large flower bed blooming with lilies of the valley. The woman finds herself strongly and joyously attracted to this yard. Consciously, she has long forgotten the wedding bouquet; however, the sight and smell evoke a feeling of romance. Her face radiates with happiness.

Feelings (Kinesthetic Sensations)

A child is put to bed after being treated by the doctor for a broken arm. He goes to sleep that night with the satin binding of a blanket tucked under his chin while his parents take turns reading him wonderful bedtime stories. After his painful ordeal, he is vastly relieved to be in his own bed with his parents present with him. Years later, he comforts himself when ill by tucking the blanket binding under his chin. He feels very peaceful and secure when he does this.

A girl goes around a gravel-paved corner fast on her bicycle. She loses control of the bicycle and takes a nasty fall. A few months later in driver education class, she finds herself feeling apprehensive when turning her car on sharp corners of gravel roads.

Sounds

A couple spend an idyllic vacation at the seashore collecting shells, swimming and snorkeling. Months later, a tape recording of sounds of the sea serves to elicit the feelings of relaxation, warmth and delight associated with the vacation. The sound of the sea heard daily on vacation has become a potent associational cue that continues to be effective even months later.

Tastes and Smells

A doctor visiting New Orleans tasted oysters for the first time. That night he became violently ill. Subsequently, the mere sight of an oyster repulsed him.

Celebrating the publication of her first novel, a young author sipped her first glass of Dom Perignon champagne in the company of close friends. Years later, the first sip of Dom Perignon still evoked those feelings of hope and "joie de vivre" she had felt on that soft spring night.

In general, associational cues are most likely to be reliable if they are connected to several senses. For example, Proust's feeling of happiness and memories were connected to the visual image of a certain kind of cookie and tea, to the smell, touch, taste, and presumably even to the sound of the cup and saucer he held in his hand. Together these sense experiences functioned as an associational cue to produce a powerful associational response.

ASSOCIATIONAL CUES WITH CHRONIC
AND RESISTANT CLIENTS

The author cannot overemphasize the therapeutic value of initially establishing the resource of a reliable associational cue for security and relaxation when working with a chronic or otherwise resistant client. Once established, this associational cue can be utilized by the therapist to:

1) establish a highly positive context for the therapeutic relation-ship, thereby minimizing resistant behavior.
2) provide a valuable resource for assisting the client in achieving integrative therapeutic changes and adjustments.

In working with chronic and resistant clients, associational cues are generally most effective and reliable if taken from the client's already existing experience. The associational cue can then, if neces-sary, be further enhanced and made more potent and reliable by repetitions incorporating additional senses.

In attempting to elicit a state of security and relaxation, it is im-portant that the therapist be in that state himself in order to avoid sending the client a contradictory nonverbal message!

Direct Strategies for Establishing
a Resource of Comfort and Security

In some instances the client's already existing cue for an expe-rience of comfort and security can be readily identified by asking him to answer in detail the question:

When and in what sorts of situations in your life have you experi-enced a deep sense of comfort and security?

For example, if a client already associates a feeling of comfort and security to a certain piece of music he used to enjoy listening to, he can be instructed to listen to the music (in actuality or in his imag-ination):

Jim, I want you to arrange yourself in the most comfortable posi-tion available to you and now go inside and really listen to that music, enjoying it as thoroughly and as vividly as you can . . . .

He can then be instructed to go back again and enjoy listening to that music while also becoming aware of the associated sights, and the feeling and position of his body that he experienced the first time the music produced the feelings of security and comfort:

> Now, return to that special music, and enjoy it vividly once more, this time noticing as you become more and more comfortable and secure . . . the position of your body, the colors and sights around you, as well as the particular sounds.

If this is repeated a number of times, the potency of the associational cue of the music will be strengthened by the client adapting a relaxed, comfortable body posture and visualizing associated inner images such as the color of the chair or objects in the room he sits in while listening to the music. Eventually, the visualized images and the client's listening body position will also become associational cues to produce the desired state.

Generally the most reliable effect will be produced by using the associational cue that incorporates three (or more) senses, such as the case of the (real or imagined) SIGHT of the chair, the (real or imagined) SOUND of the music, and the body position (FEELING) the client had when first listening to the music and feeling secure and comfortable.

Imagination and Memory Versus "Real" Experiences

With most associational cues, the memory of the cue will be as effective or almost as effective as the actual experience of the associational cue. In other words, the client's memory of the music is capable of producing the same effect as actually listening to the music.

Some Difficulties in Using Direct Strategies

When attempting to identify a client's existing associational cues for a desired feeling or response, therapists working with chronic clients are likely to encounter some who say they can never remember feeling "that way."

In other cases, asking clients to remember a time when they felt confident, comfortable and relaxed or some other desirable response may actually produce the opposite effect of making them acutely aware of all the times when they have NOT felt comfortable. This is not surprising. If chronic clients had easy conscious access to experiences of comfort, security, confidence, and other desirable feelings, they probably would not now be stuck in the rigid and often painful response patterns that characterize behavior labeled as chronic.

In explaining why she now refused to participate in structured group relaxation exercises, one client said:

The more I think about relaxing or try to remember a time when I was once relaxed, the more anxious I get. I'm starting to think I've probably never been relaxed in my life. . . . I'm a failure at that just like I'm a failure at so many other things. Trying to relax just reminds me of a lot of bad memories of all the times that I've felt terrible. . . .

Another client stated:

When you ask me about times I felt confident, secure, and relaxed, I can't even remember feeling those things singly, much less all in one experience! Trying to remember feeling that way just makes me realize how different I must be than some other people in this group. . . . It gives me this feeling that there must be something really wrong with me. . . .

In cases like these where directly talking about positive feelings serves only to elicit discomfort in the client, an indirect strategy is indicated.

INDIRECT STRATEGIES FOR
ELICITING COMFORT AND SECURITY

The Therapist's Nonverbal Communication

When attempting to elicit an experience of comfort and security in a client, the therapist should first establish that state in himself through a relaxation technique or his own favorite associational cue.

The therapist should adapt a relaxed, comfortable body posture that simultaneously conveys respect and attentiveness while communicating obvious comfort. This body posture should be shifted as often as necessary for the therapist to maintain a sense of physical ease and comfort. Moving around now and then will not detract from the feeling of relaxation being implicitly communicated to the client. Adopting a stiff, rigid posture and refusing to adjust it will! The therapist should feel free to move around, change chairs, or walk around the room if necessary.

The therapist's voice should be clearly audible, but slightly softer than a conversational tone, and just slightly slower than that used in everyday conversation.

With some clients, the therapist's implicit nonverbal communication of a state of relaxation and security will be sufficient to elicit it in the client.

> *Client*: "You always seem so peaceful and relaxed. . . . After a few minutes I start to feel that way, too. . . . (*laughing*) It's like you radiate it or something. . . .

or (client talking about a therapist)

> He's so relaxed. . . . You just get this definite feeling from him that no matter what, everything is going to be all right.

In any case, it is virtually impossible to elicit a state of comfort and security in a client if the therapist is not already congruently demonstrating it in himself! For the sake of the therapist as well as of the client, the author urges that therapists take a few minutes in between each session to relax and, metaphorically speaking, "smell the flowers." This is not self-indulgence; it is a therapeutic necessity that benefits the client as much as the therapist.

OTHER NATURALISTIC TECHNIQUES

A therapist can assist a client in establishing an associational cue for a desired response by eliciting the desired response, such as confidence and security, in the client, and then providing the client with the following indirect cues: a touch (kinesthetic), the therapist's facial expression of respect and caring (visual), and the therapist's tone of voice (auditory). The therapist's touch should be given on a nonsexual area of the body such as a shoulder or hand. If done precisely and consistently, the resulting combination of these three cues will constitute a powerful associational cue for the client to feel confident and secure in the therapy situation.

Once the client has developed confidence in her ability to have this experience in the therapy situation, she can be taught to elicit and later generalize this state to the context of everyday life outside the therapy situation.

The first step in indirectly eliciting a state of comfort and security is to discover a way to provide the client with that actual experience in the therapy situation or to vividly evoke a memory of that experience. There are several ways to accomplish this task.

"I Feel Relaxed Here with You . . . "

As stated above, some clients will respond to the therapist's state of security and relaxation by becoming relaxed and secure themselves. In other cases, a more comprehensive indirect strategy will be required.

"What Would It Be Like If You COULD
Remember Those Good Feelings?"

If the client is unable to remember feeling secure and relaxed in everyday life, the therapist may ask the client to imagine "What would it be like if you COULD remember those feelings, AS IF you had actually experienced them?" With some clients this will be effective in eliciting the desired state.

"I Once Had a Friend Who Really
Knew How to Relax . . . "

Another strategy that works with some clients is a derivation of Erickson's "My Friend John" technique (1964a). The therapist tells the client about a friend or another client who once had an experience of relaxation and security at some time in life. The therapist tells the story in rich sensory detail, emphasizing details of sight, sound, feelings, perhaps smell and taste according to known preferences of the client.

"What Do You Do For Fun?"

Some clients respond best to indirect questions about current and past activities that elicit feelings of security and relaxation. In some instances, asking a client about various activities will enable the therapist to identify a naturalistic associational cue for relaxation and security, such as "thinking about going fishing," or some other activity.

The therapist might ask the client how he likes to spend free time and observe the client's facial expression, breathing rate, and body posture to determine which experiences seem to remind the client of feelings of relaxation and security. The therapist can then engage the client in conversation about the activities that appear to generate a positive response until an experience of relaxation and security is elicited.

"I Wonder If It's Going to Rain Much This Summer . . . "

In some cases, questions even remotely connected to positive experiences or how the client is feeling emotionally will tend to elicit anxiety. Some resistant clients have earned their label by exhibiting extremely low tolerance for any question that is even remotely personal! For example:

Therapist: What do you like to do in your free time?
Client: *(anxiously)* I can't think of anything, in fact that question makes me feel how empty my life is. . . . I hate it when you shrinks ask these questions!

or, in other cases,

(angrily) None of your business!

In attempting to elicit feelings of relaxation and security with clients like the above, the therapist may have to begin by asking the client to express current feelings in a symbolic metaphorical manner, such as "How do you like this weather we're having right now?," or some other indirect query that enables the therapist to further gauge the client's current feelings.

Generally, the client's optimism or pessimism about a series of neutral topics will serve as a rough indicator of his current emotional mood and attitude about his life. For instance:

The Cubs will probably have another lousy season. . . . There's no reason to think that things are going to get any better for a long time. . . . *(pessimism, depression)*

This weather is really wonderful. . . . Maybe it will stay like this all summer. . . . *(hopefulness, possibility of growing security)*

The Olympics are disgusting! All those people who care only about their bodies and their performance . . . *(client has arms folded protectively around pot belly, apparently feels inadequate and negative about experience of discussing this topic)*

The art fair is next week. I'm going to go and get a few good books to read on weekends . . . *(resourceful, confident)*

The client's expression of feelings about fairly neutral topics such as weather, sports, and current events will supply a general context for the therapist to gauge his current level of relaxation and security, simultaneously providing a nonthreatening beginning for working with the client on establishing comfort and security. Some topics will generate more relaxation and security in the client than others, providing important information for the therapist.

The therapist can then indirectly experiment with various conversational topics until the client exhibits nonverbal expressions of comfort and security. The most reliable cues are generally the client's nonverbal unconscious responses such as relaxed body posture, relaxed facial expression, rhythmic, even breathing, and apparently relaxed tone of voice.

"Let's Go to the Park and Get Ice Cream Cones . . . "

In other cases, merely talking about an experience that is associated with relaxation and comfort will not work. With this sort of client, actually accompanying the client in activities such as a walk or an occupational therapy activity such as crafts, cooking or sports will enable the therapist to identify a naturalistic associational cue for comfort and security.

Once the therapist and client have shared an experience in which the client felt relaxed and secure, the experience can then be conversationally recalled and revivified with the therapist's presence constituting a living reminder and implicit associational cue:

Therapist: When you walked in the door just now, I found myself remembering the walk we took down by the old mill. . . .

If the therapist has difficulty in either engaging the client in a conversation about the activity or eliciting comfort and security in the client while discussing the activity, the following should be considered:

1) The client needs more experience with the therapist in the activity in order for the therapist's presence and conversation to be a powerful enough associational cue to elicit comfort and security. The activity may need to be repeated several times to establish it as a reliable associational cue.
2) The activity is not sufficiently pleasurable for the client. Another more enjoyable activity should be identified and utilized with the client to elicit comfort and security.

REFINING THE ASSOCIATIONAL CUE

Once a state of security and comfort has been elicited, the therapist can assist the client in making this state an available daily life resource by giving the client access to appropriate naturalistic or therapeutically constructed associational cues to elicit the state. In some cases, the client's awareness of *thinking about* the experience of X will suffice to teach him to elicit that state by simply thinking of the context of X in which he experienced that state in the past.

With other clients, a more specific precise associational cue or combination of cues will be required in order to make the desired state of security and comfort an available resource for the client in his everyday life where it is most likely to be needed. With this sort of client, a more conscious, structured approach will be indicated:

Systematic Approach for Refining the Associational Cue for Comfort and Security

1) Elicit that state in the client (see previously listed strategies).
2) Instruct the client to experience that state both internally and externally in all three sensory modalities: sight, sound, touch. For example: I'd like you to pay particular attention to the sights and sounds and feelings that you notice while experiencing these good feelings.
3) Instruct the client to enhance the experience by simultaneously giving himself a signal (associational cue) of a word, a touch on an easily accessible and precise part of the body (hands, arms, wrist, knees, shoulder are ideal places), and a visualized image or picture selected from his associations with the experience. Following this, invite him to select the signal that he feels is the most meaningful and appealing and have him then give himself this signal to determine if it is effective in producing this state. Repeat the above three steps until an effective and reliable associational cue is found for the desired state.

Exceptions: Finding a Way to Use the Associational Cue with "Atypical" Clients

Just as there are some clients who are unable to respond easily to direct strategies for eliciting a state of comfort and security, there will be some who will have difficulty consciously utilizing their own associational cues for positive responses.

With such a client it is best for the therapist to first identify and then indirectly use associational cues to enable the client to integrate the therapeutic response. In this way the response triggered by the associational cue will gradually and naturalistically become part of the client's everyday behavior. Feelings of comfort and security will then be available to the client as a familiar and naturalistic part of her repertoire of available responses.

Case Example

Julio was a 45-year-old client who had migrated to the United States from Italy ten years before. He suffered from paranoia and acute anxiety attacks; as a result he had difficulty working, despite his obvious desire to hold down a reliable job. At the onset of therapy he was part of a group seen by the author. The vocational rehabilitation counselor had succeeded in finding Julio a job working in a restaurant. Julio needed an associational cue that would provide him with a feeling of comfort and security in the work place. Otherwise, he was in danger of losing this job as he had all previous jobs, repeatedly leaving in a state of deep anxiety and fearfulness.

A number of questions, topics, and activities were explored with Julio in an attempt to elicit a state of security and comfort. Initially, nothing seemed to work.

After repeated attempts, the author finally succeeded in eliciting a state of deep comfort and security in Julio while preparing a dish of spaghetti with him. This *in vivo* experience of preparing spaghetti together in a group setting was repeated several times until the mention of "spaghetti" was an effective associational cue for producing a state of comfort and security.

The author then attempted to teach Julio how to elicit his own state of comfort and security by "thinking of the smells, sights, sounds, and feelings that go along with preparing and eating a good dish of spaghetti." Although the author's mention of spaghetti invariably triggered an initial state of security and comfort in Julio, asking Julio to concentrate on the sensory experiences associated with eating spaghetti seemed to take him away from the experience of comfort and security! He would become bored, restless, and then apparently anxious.

Asking Julio to concentrate on the spaghetti cue on his own produced a very different result than the associational cue of the author simply mentioning spaghetti to Julio. The author's mention of spaghetti seemed to produce a state of relaxation that would last for an hour or so. The client's own attempt to relax by "thinking of spaghetti" when not in the therapist's presence did not seem to work. The client reported that it "only makes me feel bored, then real frustrated and uptight because the good feelings don't come. . . ."

A week before the restaurant job was to begin, the author saw Julio a few minutes before a group therapy session. A fellow client asked with a smile, "Had any good spaghetti lately, Julio?" Julio brightened and obviously became relaxed and secure. The relaxation lasted throughout the group session.

The answer to Julio's difficulties became apparent. The vocational counselor could be informed of Julio's associational cue for comfort and security. Julio's supervisor at work, an understanding man, could be instructed to ask Julio each morning at the beginning of the work day, "Had any good spaghetti lately, Julio?" Julio was then able to perform his job duties without anxiety.

Eventually, Julio's feelings of comfort and security elicited by the reference to spaghetti became associated also with the work place where the supervisor had the habit of playfully and humorously asking him about the spaghetti each morning.

When the supervisor left to take another job, there was no further mention of spaghetti at work. Nevertheless, Julio's security and comfort at work continued. He had (unconsciously) integrated the experience of comfort and security into his everyday behavior at work.

The homely associational cue of "spaghetti" had served to provide Julio with the initial experiences of relaxation in the work place. Once integrated through repetition, the "spaghetti" cue was no longer necessary. Comfort and security had become a familiar part of Julio's available repertoire of ways to respond at work.

8

Reframing Chronic Symptoms—
A Utilization Approach

This chapter will illustrate direct and indirect use of associational cues in the context of a therapeutic reframing intervention.

REFRAMING: A PRIMARY UTILIZATION TECHNIQUE

Reframing is another aspect of the process in which the therapist utilizes (incorporates) the symptomatic problem behavior as part of the change strategy. The values attached to a particular behavior or perception are altered by the therapist; as a result, the client chooses to change the problem on his own.

The "reframing model," identified by Watzlawick, Weakland, and Fisch (1974), is a central part of many different therapy approaches. Reframing changes the function of a problem in such a way that it can now be employed as a positive resource for the client. Vital to the reframing approach is the therapist's acceptance and appreciation of the client's given situations, behaviors, and perceptions. The therapist achieves a high degree of rapport with the client and then utilizes the undeniable "facts" of the client's current problem to lead to less constricting, more normal behavior.

In this way, problematic relationships, behaviors, and perceptions are transformed into therapeutic resources.

To reframe something means to alter its context. For example, placing a green frame around a painting that has some, even very little, green in it will have the effect of calling attention to that color. The picture will look different than it did before the new frame was placed around it.

This chapter's case example will illustrate five steps for utilizing associational cues to reframe (alter the context and meaning) problematic perceptions and behaviors. These five steps are:

1) Establish rapport with the client.
2) Identify the client's existing naturalistic associational cue(s) for the experience of comfort and security.
3) Further develop and strengthen the client's associational cue(s) for comfort and security as needed.
4) Utilize the client's associational cue(s) for comfort and security to therapeutically alter the context and meaning attached to the problematic behaviors and perceptions.
5) Enable the client to integrate the associational cue(s) for comfort and security into daily life resources. This is accomplished by initially and then repeatedly providing this experience in the context of the therapy setting. Once this integration experience has been adequately provided, the client will independently then make further appropriate therapeutic adjustments in everyday life situations.

Case Example: Ted

Ted was a 28-year-old male client who had a chronic symptom of catatonic behavior in which he would sit completely and rigidly motionless for hours at a time, scarcely breathing. These episodes occurred two or three times each week. Ted's background included a short term in the army, from which he was discharged with a diagnosis of paranoid schizophrenia. He was treated for two years in a VA hospital because of recurring episodes in which he attempted to tear up the hospital unit in response to instructions from a hallucinated army officer. The violent acting-out behavior eventually ceased, but episodes of catatonia began to occur. Virtually any stimulus that reminded him of his experiences in the army seemed capable of triggering a catatonic response in this client.

Asked about his catatonic episodes, Ted stated, "I don't know exactly what happens. I mean I can hear everything and remember everything that happens when I'm like that, but I don't know how I get like that (catatonic)." Ted added that just before he became catatonic he experienced extreme fear. Following the fear, he reported a hallucinated army sergeant ordering him to tear up the room. At this point, Ted would begin to sob, tremble, and say brokenly, "I don't want to hurt anyone." He would then become catatonic for anywhere from one to seven hours. Ted reported that when he became catatonic he could escape from the hallucinated sergeant. It was, he said, "the only way I know how to do it."

After reorienting from the catatonic episode, Ted would be withdrawn and depressed for several days. Frequently, following one of these episodes he would attempt suicide through a low lethality overdose.

Ted's problematic pattern included: fear and anxiety, hallucination of the sergeant, a catatonic episode, and suicidal depression. This pattern had been going on for approximately four years.

His resources included average intelligence, a daughter he loved, reasonably good social skills (when he was not catatonic), some male friends in the community, a background in martial arts, and a particular fondness for going fishing. His childhood was characterized by financial hardship and abusive alcoholic parents. One of his few positive childhood memories was the experience of going fishing with his father.

1) Establishing Rapport

The author engaged Ted in conversation and rapport was established through a discussion of sports of interest to the client (topical pacing) and nonverbal symbolic communication (indirect mirroring in which the author moved her left hand in synchrony with the client's swinging legs).

2) Identifying Existing Naturalistic Associational Cues for Comfort and Security

Directly asking Ted if he recalled feeling comfortable and relaxed at any time in the past evoked no memories to serve as associational cues. However, asking him, "What do you REALLY like to do in your spare time?" led to a description of playing with his child and an animated description of a recent fishing trip they had taken together. Asked casually, "How long have you been fishing?" the client indicated that he had been going fishing since he was a young boy. Asked if there was anything else he enjoyed as a child, he said, "Sometimes hunting, but mostly fishing." "Which did you like best?" "Fishing." "Whom did you go with?" "My father when I was a kid, and now by myself or with my buddies." "Was there anything else you enjoyed doing with him or alone back then?" "Nope." "How about now?" " . . . Well, sometimes hunting, but not so much because the guns kinda bother me, remind me of the service; mostly just fishing."

A lively casual discussion then took place in which the author asked various questions and was given vivid descriptions of the fish Ted liked most to catch, some shared tales about ones that got away, and a discussion of bait and local fishing holes. In referring to another recent trip, Ted observed, "Yeah, I really like doing it. . . . It's a way to mellow out, you know, kind of give myself some space."

The author noted Ted's associations of going fishing, playing with his daughter, the words "mellowing out," "giving myself some 'space'" as potential material for associational cues. While any direct allusion to feeling relaxed and comfortable produced either no effect or an effect of mild anxiety in the client, it was discovered through a series of casual conversations between the author and Ted that indirect offhand references to fishing that engaged the client in vivid recalling of past fishing trips or imagining of potential future ones produced a response of deep relaxation and obvious comfort and security.

Conversely, the author's use of the words "mellowing out" seemed to produce no discernible effect in Ted. References to "getting some space" or "giving myself some space," however, produced an effect similar to the words "going fishing." References to "playing with your child" or playing with children sometimes produced relaxation in Ted, but occasionally evoked associations of beatings and of the things that had been missing in his relationship with his parents.

"Going fishing" and "giving yourself some 'space'" were identified as existing naturalistic associational cues for eliciting a state of deep relaxation, comfort, and security in Ted. Because of his difficulty with direct strategies for relaxation and security, he was not immediately taught directly to use his own associational cues to produce the desired state at will. Instead, an indirect approach was employed. It was for this same reason that the therapist selected existing associational cues for Ted rather than explicitly having Ted select his own signals to elicit security and relaxation.

In the day hospital program that Ted attended, he had repeatedly become catatonic, much to the consternation and fearfulness of the staff and other clients who viewed his catatonic response as a sign of imminent danger. Characteristically, people sitting near Ted quickly moved away from him as he became catatonic and fearfully implored others approaching, "Stay away from him! He's catatonic!"

Two or three days following the fishing discussion, Ted became catatonic in the day hospital group setting. The therapist observed Ted's reaction and, as the group moved away to sit at a large table across the room, said to the other clients calmly but emphatically, "That's right. It's okay to move away and that's right not to touch him because HE NEEDS TO GIVE HIMSELF SOME SPACE. HE'S TAKING SOME TIME TO GIVE HIMSELF SOME SPACE, AND THAT'S AN IMPORTANT THING TO DO." Later, as other clients approached the area where Ted was sitting, before anyone could refer to him being catatonic, the therapist again repeated, "DON'T BOTHER TED. HE NEEDS TO GIVE HIMSELF SOME SPACE."

While the above communication was overtly meant for the other clients, it constituted an indirect message to Ted. The words designated by capitals were included specifically and primarily for Ted's benefit. The staff and the people in the client group proceeded without inhibiting their everyday behavior. In this way, acceptance of Ted's symptomatic behavior was conveyed in an undeniable symbolic way.

Within an hour, Ted reoriented to the room. He appeared depressed, but was not suicidal. No reference was made to the catatonic episode or description of "giving himself some space" which had been indirectly employed as an associational cue.

The following week, Ted confided to the author his immense fear of "being catatonic and not being able to get out." The author began to search for a context from Ted's experiential world in which sitting still for a long time was a positive and not fearful activity. A review of Ted's resources led to a discussion of training techniques for karate which he had once studied. Ted mentioned that he had trained in karate several years previously, prior to his "nervous breakdown" in the service. Asked in more detail about karate, Ted said that he had liked it and that each session of his training group had begun with the students sitting and meditating in front of a candle.

Ted now described in detail the experience of meditating and elicited his own experience of comfort and security. He said he thought maybe he'd like to try meditation again. The therapist then told him: "You know, Ted, this is kind of odd, but to an outsider, when you're catatonic, the way you LOOK to someone else like me looking at you is not unlike someone who is sitting there meditating. Now that's how you look from the outside. What I want to know from you is, HOW DOES THE OUTSIDE WORLD LOOK TO YOU? In terms of the way the outside world looks when you're meditating and the way the outside world looks when you're catatonic, what are the differences?" Ted said, "The main difference I can see between the two is that in catatonia I'm scared and everyone else moves away from me and is scared of me and I feel more and more scared until finally somehow it passes and then I just feel real bad, down on myself and real scared about when this is going to happen again."

"And how is meditation different?"

"Well, I'm not scared and when I was in karate class I'd be sitting there with a bunch of other guys and of course nobody moved away from each other or got worried about what was going to happen when we were meditating."

Just prior to the next time Ted became catatonic in the day hospital setting, he began to shake and sob fearfully. The therapist asked him gently, "Do you need us to move away?" Ted said, "NO—but don't let anyone touch me." The other clients and staff were advised that "it isn't necessary to move away from Ted right now; YOU DON'T HAVE TO FEEL AFRAID OF WHAT IS HAPPENING; however, don't touch Ted right now. He needs to have some space and he's FINDing A WAY TO GET SOME SPACE for himself right now." Again, the words designated by the capitalized letters were messages meant for Ted contained within the overt communication to other clients.

Since the other clients were all very afraid of what they viewed as Ted's loss of control, there was no difficulty in ensuring that he would not be bumped, jostled or touched while in this presumably very vulnerable catatonic state. After talking with several clients who have previously been catatonic, the author surmises that the violent angry behavior that erupts with some catatonic clients when they are touched may be an extreme defensive measure indicative of their feelings of fear and vulnerability.

The client group then began to proceed as usual, with the other clients participating fully. Ted's body appeared to relax very slightly. This served, once again, to provide a message of acceptance to Ted in the context of his symptomatic behavior. Particularly in the case of working with chronically symptomatic clients, it is crucial that a therapist communicate a nonjudgmental acceptance of symptomatic behavior in order to later be able to assist the client in changing.

Characteristically, Ted's catatonic episodes were followed by a period of anxiety, depression and withdrawn behavior that would sometimes last until the next day when he became catatonic again. Previously, therapists and clients had reacted to Ted's symptom of catatonia with expressions of grave concern. In this case, the therapist and the other clients had not expressed undue concern, but instead had simply and indirectly offered reassurance of support and acceptance. This was communicated implicitly and symbolically by their remaining in close physical proximity to Ted. While no direct suggestions for comfort and security were offered at this time, a feeling of security and safety was conveyed through the therapist's relaxed body posture and comfortable tone of voice. The catatonic behavior was now seen as a way for Ted to ''give himself some space.'' In this way, Ted's associational cue of giving himself some space was utilized to place a new frame of meaning around the symptomatic catatonic behavior.

Within about 20 minutes, Ted appeared to be beginning to reorient to the room. At this point the therapist asked him to nod or shake his head if there was anything he wanted. Ted made a slight nodding motion, but was unable to verbalize. He was told, ''You can take as much time as you need to tell us, Ted, and you can rest assured that we'll be here for you if you need us.''

After several more minutes, Ted's head trembled slightly with apparent spasms in the muscles of his neck. He said, ''I'm just so scared. . . . Please don't let anyone touch me—I'm afraid I'll lose control of myself.'' The therapist reassured, ''Don't worry, Ted, no one will touch you. Maybe you need to give yourself some more 'space.''' Ted nodded and looked more relaxed. The therapist then told him, ''While you're doing that I'm going to continue with the group. Every now and then I'm going to look at you and I will depend on you to let me know by nodding if there is anything you need. Be sure to take as much 'space' as you need, and don't worry about coming out until you really feel ready. We're here with you.''

By being directed to continue to give himself ''space'' until he felt ready to come out, Ted was given some initial control of his catatonic symptom. This strategy of initially directing a client to continue to experience his existing symptom is described by Erickson as ''symptom prescription.'' In Ted's case, symptom prescription simultaneously enhanced the reframing of catatonia as a way of giving himself some space in order to cope positively with feelings of fear and anxiety. Telling him to continue until he felt ''ready to come out'' also constituted an implicit therapeutic reassurance that he would indeed eventually be able to reorient to the room.

After about an hour, Ted reoriented to the room. Unlike in other instances of catatonic episodes, he was able to almost immediately begin talking to other people and begin to participate in some group activities, although in a quiet and passive manner.

Since Ted's peers in the client group had not been directed to move away from him during the catatonic episode, they knew by implication that what he had done was not something to fear. Therefore, when he reoriented they began to comfortably ask him how he was now feeling and what he had been experiencing. This behavior on the part of his peers further enhanced the reframing of Ted's symptomatic catatonic behavior.

Asked how he was feeling, Ted said he had been uncomfortable and very fearful, "like I usually am when I'm like that." The difference between this episode and other episodes was not how Ted experienced the catatonia but rather the length of the episode and the degree of Ted's ability to communicate and interact socially following the episode. The fact that Ted had in fact taken in the therapeutic meaning of the author's allusion to "he's just giving himself some space" was demonstrated later in the day when a client who had left the room for an appointment returned several hours later and asked Ted if he was all right. Ted replied, "Yeah, I'm okay. I was just giving myself some SPACE. I'm okay now."

Ted's ability to interact with others and to care for himself improved following the indirect utilization of his associational cue of giving himself some "space" and the positive context provided by people around him remaining secure and relaxed. Two weeks later there had been only one brief episode of catatonia. The therapist and the other clients had responded in the same relaxed accepting manner. Ted had made no further suicide gestures and appeared to be in reasonably good spirits. He had become more active in the group setting and was spending more time talking to other clients and staff.

A subsequent discussion with Ted, however, disclosed that he was not entirely okay, that he still feared and dreaded becoming catatonic again. While he had not experienced any hallucinations of the army sergeant for the week following the previous episode, he still feared that these hallucinations could come back even though he said, "I know in my head the sergeant isn't real, but in my guts he IS real and it scared the hell out of me."

As demonstrated by a shortened but recent catatonic episode, Ted was still suffering from the catatonic states over which he felt he had little control. It was clear that, although his symptom had been slightly ameliorated, a more complete intervention was needed.

In addition, Ted was particularly concerned about a trip he was taking to a nearby city with several old school chums who were likely to bring up a discussion of subjects related to their experiences in the armed services—"The kind of things," Ted said, "that really set me off." And yet, Ted was not willing to give up this four-hour trip in an old van with his buddies who were, in his words, "the best friends I've ever had." The trip was a month away.

3) Further Developing and Strengthening Existing Associational Cues for Comfort and Security

The therapist continued to spend some casual conversational time individually with Ted each day to further develop rapport and to learn as much as possible about Ted's existing associational cues for security and comfort. It was learned that, in addition to going fishing with his father, he frequently, as a young boy, had also gone fishing alone. He had greatly enjoyed the experience, feeling very peaceful, calm and relaxed, sometimes sitting on an old dock, sometimes sitting in a small boat amid the quiet ripples of the water.

It was also learned that he more recently, as an adult, had enjoyed walks in a small scented pine forest near his home on the way to a favorite fishing spot at a nearby stream. Once there, he would sit, relaxed and calm, on the banks of the stream, listening to the wind in the trees and the gurgling of the water. Thinking about going fishing on his walk en route through the forest also had become an experience of peace and deep security.

When he vividly described these sensory experiences to the therapist, Ted reexperienced the deep security, relaxation and comfort associated with the experience of going fishing. The therapist then invited Ted: "Why not take a few minutes right now to really enjoy that experience, to really enjoy what it means for you when you spend some time just 'thinking about going fishing'?''

Each day the therapist spent some informal individual time with Ted, casually asking him to recall in detail his favorite fishing experience, paying attention to all the sights and sounds and feelings and "noticing how you felt just before you reached that favorite fishing hole, that anticipation of thinking about going fishing, and then later on remembering that fish you caught and sometimes the one that you enjoyed almost catching, all those good memories that go with 'thinking about going fishing.'''

Averting potential resistance. The second day the therapist asked Ted to recall going fishing, Ted looked quizzical. The therapist responded to this honestly by telling him, "I'm not sure why or how yet, but I have a strong feeling that this is very valuable and important for you." This seemed to satisfy Ted completely. The therapist's respectful honesty was crucial at this point in reassuring the client that his interests were held at heart.

Refining the associational cue. The procedure of asking Ted to describe in detail his sensory associations with favorite fishing trips was repeated daily. Each day, at the end of the descriptions, Ted was then asked to "take some time for yourself to enjoy what it means to be 'thinking about going fishing.'''

By the end of two weeks, "thinking about going fishing" constituted a powerful associational cue for Ted to elicit a deep feeling of comfort and security. The actual words, "comfort," "security," and "relaxation" were not directly employed with Ted because of his previous difficulty with direct relaxation techniques. Instead, the effect of the associational cue was tested by repeatedly asking Ted to spend a minute or two thinking about going fishing and then "come back and let me know how you're feeling." Always, Ted reported feeling "mellow, good, like everything is all right." The therapist tested the effectiveness of this strategy by deliberately bringing up some subjects that were aversive to Ted, such as thinly veiled references to the army and allusions to his catatonia. Ted was then directed to "take a minute to think about going fishing."

Ted's body would visibly relax, his breathing deepen, and he reported feeling "mellow, . . . good, all right." It was also observed that Ted repeatedly and reliably exhibited these same minimal physical cues of relaxed body posture and deep relaxed breathing in response to the therapist talking about going fishing or fishing experiences. At this point, "thinking about going fishing" constituted a reliable associational cue for Ted's feelings of comfort and security.

4) Utilizing an Associational Cue to Reframe a Catatonic Symptom

After three weeks of careful observation, the following naturalistic strategy was employed to assist Ted in utilizing an associational cue as a therapeutic resource in the context of his catatonic symptom.

The therapist wanted to connect the experience of security and relaxation that Ted associated with thinking about going fishing to the catatonic state in such a way as to alter the context and meaning of that symptomatic state. Since the treatment issue was too important to risk possible failure through an approach that was too direct to be acceptable to Ted, the appropriate associational cues were provided in an indirect fashion.

The therapist waited until Ted predictably became catatonic in the group treatment setting. The therapist then began a casual discussion with the other client group members regarding favorite leisure time pursuits. The therapist knew from experience with the individuals in this group that the discussion would inevitably turn to fishing. Although Ted was the acknowledged expert on fishing in the group, several of the other people were active in the sport. The group members began to spontaneously talk about favorite fishing spots, telling stories about fish they had caught, and hopes and plans for future fishing trips. The therapist reflected, "It really is nice to SPEND SOME TIME THINKING ABOUT GOING FISHING." She then invited all the group members to "take a little more time right now to really enjoy remembering some of the best times you've had going fishing."

5) Integration of an Associational Cue as a Therapeutic Resource

Following these two directives, Ted's breathing rate changed and he made several small shifts in his body posture. He then reoriented to the group and immediately began to talk casually about fishing in a relaxed, agreeable manner, as if nothing had happened. This was a major change from his usual anxiety and passivity following a catatonic episode.

No comment was made regarding the change in Ted's behavior following the catatonic episode. The therapist feared that Ted might begin to consciously analyze the experience in response to a comment from the therapist, and this might in turn interfere with the therapeutic change process. Ted had no apparent conscious awareness of how he had reoriented so quickly or of the fact that he had previously been in a catatonic state.

The following week, Ted took his anticipated trip to a distant city with his male friends. They rode together in a small van. Ted later gave the following account of the experience. During the ride, the other men began telling long detailed stories about various experiences they each had in the service. Ted said,

> It was terrible. They kept talking about the army and the navy and the marines and I kept trying to change the subject, but they just kept talking. I knew that if this kept up, the sergeant would come and I'd get catatonic. . . . So I kept thinking about going fishing, and I'd get all calmed down and then they'd tell another army story, and I didn't know what to do. I was starting to get scared again and I just couldn't explain about all this to them . . . they'd think I was nuts. So I'd think about fishing again and I'd be all right. I was worried because I knew I was going to have to get catatonic sometime and I was afraid it would "freak" them out. I didn't want to scare them. . . . So I waited until we stopped by the side of the road to take a leak, and I walked off by myself for a few minutes, maybe 10 or 15, and was catatonic. They thought I was taking a shit (laughs) and they made some jokes about me being gone so long. . . . But I didn't say nothin' because they'd never understand, they'd think I was loony.

Ted said he had managed fine for the rest of the two-day trip, but once or twice a day he had to find a place and time to become catatonic for a few minutes. He managed to do this in a variety of ways, all ingeniously designed to avoid causing his friends worry or discomfort.

For instance, Ted had pretended to be going to sleep just before he sensed that he would need to become catatonic for a few minutes. He had come out of his catatonia feeling comfortable and secure: "I gave myself some 'space.'" On the long drive home, his friends had drunk some beer in the back of the van and the stories became more and more vivid. Ted said he had to become catatonic twice in order to survive this experience and prevent the sergeant from coming. By managing to steer the conversation towards fishing a couple of times (using his own associational cue), taking a nap in the van (catatonia), and stopping by the road to go to the bathroom (catatonia), he avoided any difficulties or embarrassment. Because the other men were in a hurry to get home and he didn't want to inconvenience them, Ted said he was "able" to become catatonic by the side of the road for only about five minutes. Ted said that the sergeant had not come during the trip, but only because he became catatonic and "gave myself some space" to prevent it.

When he got home, Ted went into the bathroom at home and stayed there for about 15 minutes during which he finished being catatonic, giving himself some "space." During this time, his wife presumably thought he was taking a bath, which he in fact was also doing! While this was a somewhat long time to tie up the only bathroom in the house and therefore may have slightly annoyed his wife, it certainly did not occasion the discomfort that would have occurred if her husband had exhibited his previous four or five hours of catatonia.

Following this incident, Ted began to attend the day treatment program less and less, showing up strictly on an "as needed" basis about once a month. Repeatedly he would relate to the therapist how he had "fooled" someone into thinking he was "just regular" when actually he was having a catatonic episode at the moment.

Ted's strategies became more and more comfortable and ingenious. For example, he said that sometimes he would deliberately steer the conversation towards fishing so that he was then able to be catatonic and yet be perfectly able to talk and move around during the episode. He said, "I can talk fine, but my humor isn't as good."

Ted then discovered that he could talk about other things while he was in the catatonic state and still remain fairly comfortable as long as they were things he enjoyed talking about, topics that made him feel calm and relaxed. When these strategies didn't work, he made an excuse to go "meditate," take a bath, or go to the bathroom at his first opportunity. Since there were some marital issues between Ted and his wife, she wasn't always thoughtful enough to leave him alone while he "meditated." Therefore, he frequently had to resort to the bathroom technique. In the kinds of emergency situations that occur when several people share one bathroom, Ted could now shorten his catatonic episode to just a minute or two if necessary!

The last time the author saw Ted he had recently purchased a small house and had embarked in a small business endeavor. He told me that he had learned to fool people so well that they couldn't tell he was catatonic when he actually was. The author asked him if he really thought he actually was catatonic in those instances, and he said he felt he really was, even though, when he had to, he could carry on a conversation in that state. He said, "But my body is a little shaky and jerky at those times and jokes don't seem as funny."

The last report the author had regarding Ted was that his attempt at small business had failed and that he continued to have some marital issues with his wife who refused to come in with him for counseling. He continued to live in the house he had purchased and was looking for a job.

Ted continues to attend the day treatment program on an "as needed" basis, sometimes going for months without attending the program and other months attending for several days to find structure and support. He still obviously has some difficulties to iron out. He has recurring conflicts in his marriage and sometimes he annoys his family by spending too much time in the bathroom or locked in his bedroom "meditating." However, the problem description of a man who is currently unemployed, likes to talk about fishing, meditates, and sometimes takes too long in the bathroom is far less debilitating than the clinical diagnosis of chronic and paranoid schizophrenia with episodes of catatonia, psychotic depression and recurrent suicide attempts.

Discussion

No attempt was made to totally do away with Ted's remaining symbolic symptom of catatonia, once it became sufficiently manageable to enable Ted to carry out his daily life in the community. The author believes that with clients like Ted the symptom is likely to play a needed protective role for the client and should not be removed without great caution. For instance, Ted, although a former abused child himself, does not abuse his own child. The catatonic symptom may be one of the resources he uses to protect himself and his child from violent impulses.

Summary of Intervention
(Using Associational Cues to Reframe Symptoms)

The following steps were taken:

1) *Establish rapport with client.* This was accomplished in Ted's case through topical pacing, talking about sports, fishing and things Ted found interesting, and a series of casual conversations that repeatedly communicated the therapist's continuing interest and respect.

2) *Identify client's existing associational cues for comfort and security.* This was accomplished with Ted by finding out what he most enjoyed doing and then determining what emotional states were elicited by his recalling his favorite activities from the past and present. Ted's associational cues for comfort and security included "giving myself some space" and "going fishing."

3) *Further develop and strengthen client's existing associational cues until they constitute a reliable resource for eliciting comfort and security.*

This was accomplished with Ted by repeatedly asking him to think about going fishing and recall favorite fishing experiences. The strength and reliability of the associational cue, "thinking about going fishing," was tested by the therapist interspersing various negative contexts, such as allusions to the military, in between "thinking about going fishing." This was done to ensure that negative contexts would not later cancel out the effect of the associational cues at times when Ted was likely to need it most.

4) *Utilize client's associational cues to change the context of (reframe) problematic behaviors and perceptions.* This was accomplished with Ted through the therapist's descriptions of catatonia as a way to "give himself some space," nonverbal communication of a calm, secure context through the therapist's calm, relaxed voice tone, and body posture. Ted's associations with meditating in karate training were also utilized by the therapist who first discussed this with Ted and then directed other clients to not be afraid or move away from Ted while he was catatonic.

5) *Enable the client to integrate the associational cue into his daily life as an available resource.* This was accomplished by first providing the integrative experience in the therapy context, in which the therapist connected the associational cue for comfort and security, "thinking about going fishing," to Ted's symptomatic problem state by having a conversation that included and emphasized "thinking about going fishing" take place in Ted's presence while he was in the symptomatic catatonic state. The associational cue for comfort and security then became reliably linked to Ted's symptomatic catatonic state and was available to him at the times when he most needed the resource of security and comfort. Once this experience had been adequately provided, Ted then began to make further therapeutic adjustments on his own, using the associational cue of "thinking about going fishing" as a way to transform his catatonia into a coping mechanism.

9

Metaphors: Communicating with Chronic and Resistant Clients Through Stories

Metaphors are one of the hallmarks of the Ericksonian approach to therapy. Erickson used personal anecdotes to motivate, to generate new perceptions and behaviors, to overcome limitations, and as a teaching tool (Rosen, 1982). This chapter will focus on the metaphorical aspects of chronic and resistant clients' communication and will provide a practical step-by-step model for constructing and using therapeutic metaphors.

AN EXPERIENTIAL PRELUDE

A Metaphor for Metaphors

Welcome to the land of process communication: a richly rewarding and fruitful if somewhat hilly and curvy terrain. The vast potential for utilization available in the context of metaphors in relation to the psychotherapeutic process is best conveyed by having you imagine that you are now standing in the middle of an immense and beautiful hallway. You slowly and comfortably begin to walk down the hallway, enjoying a feeling of deep security. On one side of the hallway are all the things that delight you. On the far opposite side are the things that you dislike.

There are portraits on the walls of all the people who have been in your life, whom you would like to be in your life in the future, and all those people you have missed having in your life up until this moment. There are symbols chosen from the depths of your unconscious representing all the relationships you hope to have, will have, have had, and might have had with yourself, with others, and with experiential learnings. Wishes, dreams, hopes, and fears are all grouped evocatively on the walls. You then notice that the walls are lined with mirrors. There are mirrors within mirrors within mirrors. And you begin to see yourself and experience yourself comfortably and interestingly in a variety of new contexts. You realize that YOU REALLY DO have EVERY-THING YOU NEED TO FULLY and MAGNIFICENTLY BE WHO-ever YOU ARE. There is an infinitely wide and complex array of possibilities for surprise and delight as well as for all other emotions, relationships, and experiences. Knowing that, and experiencing it fully, you now begin to appreciate the fact that you are NOW ALERT, REFRESHED AND RELAXED, and ready to further explore the concept of metaphorical communication.

METAPHORS: THE MIRROR WITHIN THE MIRROR

A metaphor is defined as a "figure of speech in which a term is transferred from one object it ordinarily designates to an object it may designate only by implicit comparison or analogy" (Webster's Unabridged Dictionary). A metaphor is something that stands for that which it is not. Process metaphors are metaphors in which the analogy is provided by behavior or relationship rather than solely by words.

As stated in the prelude to this chapter, trying to describe the rich and vast potential for therapeutic utilization available in the context of metaphorical communication is best conveyed by the sensory image of looking down a hall of mirrors. Metaphors provide mirrors within mirrors within mirrors for the therapeutic process involved. An exhaustive discussion of the therapeutic use of metaphors could fill several volumes. This chapter will therefore focus specifically on metaphor as a concept and as a technique for working with chronic and resistant clients.

METAPHOR AS PROCESS COMMUNICATION

Every piece of verbal and nonverbal communication is an implicit metaphor for the communicator's inner process. Clients, no matter how "resistant" or "uncommunicative" they may appear on a direct verbal level, are invariably screaming out their current issues and concerns on a metaphorical process level. Every piece of communication is potentially a process metaphor for the way the client currently experiences the relationship with himself and with other people in his world.

Listening to the Client's Metaphorical Communication

The therapist's direct attempts to learn about family interactions or emotional experiences behind a client's presenting problem of anxiety or depression may be unsuccessful. Some "resistant" clients typically communicate an outward stoicism by the content of their words, e.g., "I don't want to hang my dirty laundry on the line." Yet the client is in the therapist's office and presumably wants relief from the symptom. The tone of voice and body language indicate that the client is feeling depression or, perhaps, anxiety or anger. At the moment the client is unwilling or perhaps unable to face talking about that feeling directly.

What does the therapist do?

Ideally, the therapist will eventually achieve enough rapport to enable the client to explore those issues and feelings directly in the therapy session. However, in the process of achieving rapport, the therapist can create a metaphorical context that allows the client to express the PROCESS of what is going on inside him or her indirectly, METAPHORICALLY. The therapist can then ask the client about virtually any neutral conversation topic and the way the client responds will provide an indication of the client's current process pattern in relation to self and others. In this way, the therapist will get a general idea of how the client is dealing with current life issues.

For example a therapist the author knew in Wisconsin would often talk about the "weather" with the farmers he was seeing for therapy. He would talk with them about the Farmers Almanac and they would discuss the crops and the predicted weather, as well as the recent and distant past weather and what this portended for the next few days, weeks, months, and years. The way the farmer described his perceptions about weather, the farm economy, and the soil he had to work with would generally provide a good indication of the characteristics of relationships in the client's current personal life, and what sorts of feelings he was likely to have attached to his current situation.

Later, when rapport was more fully established, the therapist would further explore feelings and issues with the client. Invariably, the client's process level stories about weather and farming conditions contained an apt metaphorical description of what was going on in his personal life.

While the above strategy is suited to the rural client, similar metaphorical communications are provided by urban clients spontaneously or in response to the therapist's casual questions about gardens, weather, seasons, popular music, or other topics. Regardless of the precise content of the story, the client's tone and gestures while telling stories provide an accurate indication of the current emotional state.

Whatever feeling a person is experiencing at the moment will color everything he or she says and does. Verbal and nonverbal expressions and their absence can all be viewed as pieces of metaphorical communication from the client. Friendly casual conversation provides an excellent context for therapists to elicit metaphorical process communication from clients while simultaneously establishing rapport. The fact that this is mutually enjoyable further enhances the quality of the therapeutic relationship.

Eliciting and Understanding Metaphorical Communication

For the purpose of eliciting metaphorical communication that is indicative of the client's basic process patterns, it is best to steer the conversation to neutral general topics that are not likely to be loaded with implicit emotional values in and of themselves. For instance, a client's comment about the death of a loved one or the politics of nuclear war will tend to have more to do with his reac-

tion to that particular topic rather than constituting an apt metaphorical reflection of his way of relating to others and to himself.

General everyday topics like the weather, sports, hobbies, and
travel experiences are usually useful in eliciting metaphors regarding the client's general process of interacting with the world and
self. How the client interacts with the therapist, how he asks, an-
swers and doesn't answer questions, how he breathes, moves, sits,
his way of interacting with all the other people in his world, all these
are metaphors for the way he is in relation to himself—his inner
process.

Children tend to be wonderful at intuitively comprehending process level metaphorical communication. Children can be with someone for a few minutes and know whether they "like" that person
or not. They pick up "vibrations" from the way the person does
whatever he happens to be doing at the moment.

Adults, on the other hand, tend to get distracted by the explicit
meaning of the words being said, ignoring all the minimetaphors
in the person's voice tone, speech rhythm, and body movements,
and the implicit meaning of what is actually being said and not said.
As therapists, we have the obligation of reinheriting the wisdom
of seeing with a child's eyes. There is no such thing as an uncommunicative client, and to that extent there is no such thing as a resistant client. The limits are the therapist's ability to stretch far
enough to meet the client in the client's metaphorical model of the
world in order to truly hear what the client is communicating. This
demands that the therapist find a way to suspend or move beyond
his own issues in order to fully accept the client. Inevitably there
will be times when the therapist is unable to do this.

As human beings, we each have personal limits. The therapist
who has integrity will be willing to face the fact that he is at times
unable to stretch far enough beyond his current limits to fully understand and experience the metaphorical communication he is receiving from the client. At times, the very act of facing a limitation
will enable the therapist to move beyond it.

Realizing that virtually every aspect of a person's behavior is a
metaphor for his internal process, "resistant," "withdrawn," or
"uncommunicative" behavior becomes less frustrating and irritat-

ing to the therapist. It no longer constitutes a personal power strug-
gle. The client isn't defying the therapist. Rather, the client is communicating a sense of fear, anger, loneliness, grief, hopelessness, or
other emotion. "Resistant" behavior is symptomatic of the client's
current internal issues. It can and should be appreciated by the therapist as a valuable and succinct form of communication. It is a metaphor for the process issues the client brings to therapy.

METAPHOR AS TECHNIQUE: STORIES AND ANECDOTES

Stories and anecdotes provide an enjoyable and naturalistic way
for therapists to communicate with resistant clients who are unable
to respond to more direct techniques. Storytelling enables the therapist to send process level therapeutic messages to the client. If a
metaphor is appropriately constructed and skillfully told in a context of deep rapport, the client will readily respond to the message
on an unconscious level.

The Self-Referential Search

The nature of the therapeutic relationship contributes to the effectiveness of metaphors. Since the story or anecdote is being told
to the client by a therapist, the implication is that the story is meaningful and will ultimately be useful to the client. When the story
or anecdote is vague in its direct applicability while still being
isomorphic to the client's situation, the client is impelled to search
inside himself to find an appropriate meaning to assign to the
story.

The client derives meaning from the metaphor through a review of his own resources and experiences to meet the therapeutic requirement. The exact meaning the client attaches to the
story is derived from the client's own inner resources: memories,
dreams, goals, previous experiences, fantasies, hopes, fears, unconscious learning. Because the meaning is based on the client's
inner resources, the resulting application will fit the client's needs
exactly.

Creating a Therapeutic Metaphor

Creating and skillfully telling an absorbing story is an art in itself. However this does not mean that the therapist has to be a "born" storyteller or a professional novelist to master this skill and use it effectively with clients!

When telling stories and anecdotes to assist clients in therapeutic change, it is not essential that the stories be highly sophisticated and polished. It is far more important that the stories be told in a context of deep therapeutic rapport, in a naturalistic and interesting manner, and that the stories contain an accurate metaphorical representation of the client's general process patterns of thinking and behaving. To the extent that the metaphor reflects both the client's general process patterns and life situation, it will be isomorphic to the client, and potently therapeutic.

The most crucial precondition for successful use of metaphor as a therapeutic technique is achieving adequate rapport with the client. The therapist can then develop an understanding and appreciation for the client's specific daily life issues as well as a general process level representation of the client's problematic ways of perceiving and behaving.

Identifying Process Patterns

In achieving an understanding of the relationship patterns that characterize a client's process of behaving and perceiving, it is useful to make a list of verbs and adverbs that describe the client's current problem.

For example, a client might request therapy because he is experiencing symptoms of severe depression, including sleeplessness, anxiety, and difficulty attending to tasks. When asked what he is feeling depressed about, the client states that he is still feeling attached to a woman who divorced him five years ago. He says, "I just can't seem to 'let go' of her." He continues to call her on the phone, waiting until she "hangs up" on him. He "hangs on" to old memories about the former relationship. Despite her angry rebuffs, he continues to make a nuisance of himself. While he thinks about dating other women, he feels unable to "let" himself "go" out with them because of fears that they will reject him.

In the above case, the process patterns of the client's problem involve "hanging on" and "letting go." While the specific content of the issues the client is experiencing on an interpersonal level (fighting with his ex-wife, feeling afraid to go out with other women, feeling depressed and distracted because of this) will differ from the content of the intrapersonal problems of the client (anxiety, insomnia, short attention span), on a process level they will tend to be the same.

On an intrapersonal level, the client is experiencing tension and anxiety. He feels unable to "let go" and relax. He continues to "hang on" to old negative beliefs about his personal adequacy, thereby preventing himself from developing more confident and rewarding ways of viewing himself intrapersonally and interacting with others interpersonally.

On both an interpersonal and an intrapersonal level, the process patterns here involve themes of "hanging on" and "letting go." The client is stuck in the first part of the pattern sequence, "hanging on."

Constructing a Metaphor

This client could be told a metaphor about "hanging on" and "letting go" involving an individual in some way indirectly resembling himself. By reflecting the process patterns rather than the specific content of the client's problem, the metaphor remains isomorphic to the client without risking embarrassment or eliciting resistance from the client by being too direct.

The metaphorical story should include a symbolic representation of the following:

1) the client's current PROBLEM situation;
2) the client's HOPE (the desired therapy outcome);
3) the client's OBJECTION to achieving desired state;

4) MOTIVATION (an exaggeration of the client's worst feared consequences of failing to achieve the desired therapeutic change);
5) An UNANTICIPATED RESOURCE (introduction of a new or previously overlooked element);
6) A CHANGE related to the resource but occurring in a way that could not have been originally predicted, culminating in the desired state;
7) REGRESSION to the problem state utilized to lead back to and further enhance the desired therapeutic outcome.

The client was told the following anecdote:

1) A friend of mine from Nebraska decided to learn to water ski one summer. In Nebraska they create lakes by making dams and flooding an old gravel pit or canyon. HE WAS STUCK in a small Nebraska town for the summer and learning to water ski seemed like a good idea.

2) My friend had seen other people ski on the manmade lake near his family's house; now he wanted to EXPERIENCE the obvious FEELINGS OF FREEDOM AND PLEASURE OF MOVING CONFIDENTLY along the bright blue surface of the water, feeling the spray from the waves, and the refreshing lake breeze.

3) So he made arrangements to be pulled by a motorboat. Putting on his skis, HE WONDERED IF HE WOULD FALL and break one of his legs as his cousin had done the year before. His cousin was a seasoned water skier.

4) On the other hand, my friend was 15 years old and bored to tears in that small lake community. He NEEDED TO LEARN TO DO SOMETHING NEW OR HE FEARED HE WOULD "DIE" FROM BOREDOM AND LONELINESS. You can rest assured, Jerry, (*client's name*) that life can be tedious for a 15-year-old in a small town.

5) Getting up on the water skis was surprisingly easy, and he had almost made it around the lake when the driver of the boat swerved suddenly to avoid hitting two young GIRLS in a rowboat. Afterwards, he wasn't sure whether the fall was caused by the sudden change in direction or the sight of two PRETTY GIRLS watching him! He fell into the water and began to get dragged along by the tow rope, hanging on for dear life and gasping for breath as the water poured over his face and body. One ski had fallen off and was floating in the distance on the water. All he was thinking was, "I want to get back up." The girls kept screaming something to him, and it took a while before he figured out what they were saying to him:

6) "LET GO of the rope": He did EXACTLY THAT and soon was aboard the boat. A few minutes later he was skiing again and FULLY ENJOYING himself.

7) That summer as YOU and I could realistically predict, JERRY MY FRIEND MIGHT COMFORTABLY FALL AGAIN NOW AND THEN, only to remember the pretty girls and the words "LET GO OF THE ROPE." He would let go, move back into position and TRY AGAIN. He would keep trying. HE REALLY LEARNED to ski that summer. Now at age 33 he still skis well and HAS CONFIDENTLY taught MANY FRIENDS.

A few weeks after this metaphor was told to the client, he noticed that he had "forgotten" to call his ex-wife as he usually did. He casually reported to the therapist that he had gone out on dates with two different "pretty" women in the past week on a friendly informal basis. His symptoms of anxiety and depression had disappeared. A year later, the client had contacted his ex-wife only once, regarding legal business, and was comfortably participating in social activities with friends of both sexes. He described a close and pleasurable relationship with his current girlfriend, and appeared happy and well-adjusted.

ANALYSIS OF THE METAPHOR

Content

The client particularly liked outdoor sports and had an affinity for boats and water, although he did not know how to ski. Topical pacing was achieved by incorporating the water sports subjects into the story in a naturalistic fashion. The client's most highly favored representational system was kinesthetic. Therefore, words describing the "feeling" of water skiing were inserted to enhance the appeal of the story: i.e., "feeling the spray," water "pouring" on his face, etc. Kinesthetic predicates were used whenever appropriate.

Metaphorical Representations

1) *Current problem.* The client's current PROBLEM situation was represented in the word "stuck," and the reference to water being dammed up inside an old gravel pit (emotions locked into the old relationship with his ex-wife).

2) *Desired therapy outcome—the client's hope.* The client's HOPE was represented by references to the "friend" wanting to "experience feelings" of "pleasure" and "confident movement."

3) *Client's objections.* The client's possible or actual OBJECTIONS to achieving his therapeutic goal were represented by the "friend" worrying that he might "fall" and "break one of his legs" after learning to water ski. Objections are often seen in the form of fears about possible negative consequences of achieving the desired state. It is always important to account for the client's potential objections. Every symptomatic problem behavior has or once had some purpose; as a result, the client is likely to have an objection to giving it up. This objection may be on an unconscious or conscious level, or both, and is likely to be present even if the client consciously finds it highly inconvenient and annoying to hang onto the problem.

4) Motivation. The reference to the "friend" "fearing" he would "die" from "boredom and loneliness" unless he "learned to do something new" represents an exaggeration of the client's worst fears regarding the consequence of not achieving the desired therapeutic goal. The purpose of this is to increase the client's MOTIVATION to be willing to take the risk of attempting the therapeutic change. It constitutes a warning regarding the worst that could befall the client as a consequence of not attempting the change the client desires. The reference to the friend "fear(ing)" he might "die" of "loneliness" if he did not "learn to do something new" serves to represent the client's despair and possible suicidal thoughts, thus strongly motivating him to come up with a solution.

5) Unanticipated resource (introduction of a new or previously overlooked element). The "girls" represented a previously overlooked and therefore "new" RESOURCE: the client's inherent ability to develop new and rewarding relationships both in terms of his way of relating to himself (intrapersonal) and establishing new relationships with others (interpersonal). He could develop a more positive way of looking at himself and he could create rewarding relationships with people to satisfy his healthy needs for closeness and intimacy. In order to bypass his old patterns of despair and conscious fears, it is essential that the resource be represented as something new or previously overlooked. This causes the client to make an unconscious search for a previously overlooked or newly acquired resource in his daily life experience.

6) The therapeutic change. "Letting go of the rope" and "fully enjoying" represent the actual therapeutic CHANGE that occurs in a way that could not have been predicted at the beginning of the story. The change results from an interaction with the new resource (5). The element of unpredictability and/or surprise is crucial here because that detail dictates that the solution must be something that the client has not already consciously identified or has unsuccessfully tried. This enables the client to spontaneously bypass any conscious interference to resolving the problem. In the actual case example, the client simply "happened to forget" to telephone his ex-wife. He reported that he "just happened" to ask two pretty girls out the next week. The client described the experience as, "I just found myself doing it and I was surprised first that I was doing it and then surprised at how comfortable I was feeling." Later, the client "noticed" in retrospect that he was no longer feeling depressed.

7) Regression (for future integration). This element ensures that the therapeutic change will be lasting. The reference to the "friend" falling "again now and then" represents the client's predictable regression to his old problem state. Predictably there will be times when this client will again feel lonely, inadequate and depressed. He is likely to think about his ex-wife again at some time.

In the therapeutic metaphor, the client's predictable regression is represented as part of a sequence that leads directly back to the therapeutic change process. "Falling" (back into old patterns) in the metaphor leads to thinking about "pretty girls" (resource depicting new relationships for client) and "trying again." This eventually leads to an integrative experience where the client "really learns," represented in the story as "really learning to ski."

A final reference is made in the story to "confidence" and sharing what he has learned, "teaching water skiing," with "many friends." The reference to "many friends" represents an invitation to the client to continue to develop positive and rewarding relationships in the future and can be interpreted both in terms of being a better friend to himself and establishing friendships with others. This section of the metaphor provides an unconscious suggestion to the client to ensure continuing therapeutic integration. The indirect suggestions for integration contained in this last section were given added emphasis by inserting the client's name, and employing the word, "you" to secure the client's attention.

It is not essential that a therapeutic metaphor be told in the exact sequence above; however, it should contain a representation of the above seven elements in order to ensure effectiveness. In addition to the structure and content of the story, therapeutic effectiveness is also enhanced by the *manner* in which the metaphor is delivered.

EFFECTIVELY TELLING THE THERAPEUTIC METAPHOR

As in every other therapeutic interaction, metaphorical stories and anecdotes will be most effective if told to the client in a context of deep rapport. While telling the story or anecdote, the therapist should be nonverbally communicating deep acceptance and rapport. Nonverbal pacing by matching the client's body movements and postures is useful for this purpose. It is also useful for the therapist to match predicates to the client's most favored representational system: kinesthetic, visual, or auditory. Topical pacing is also desirable. This enables the therapist to "speak the client's language."

While telling the metaphor, it is important to gauge tone, style, and content to the client's ongoing nonverbal reactions. The therapist should watch for ideomotoric head nods, small body movements, minute shifts in posture, minimal or marked shifts in breathing patterns, and eye movements. Predictably there will be certain themes and content, as well as delivery styles, that will elicit a stronger response from the client. A good reason for the therapist to tell a series of stories rather than just one is that this allows the therapist to quickly drop content or themes that the client is not responding to. The therapist can then expand on the themes and content that appear to elicit a stronger response.

Choosing an Appropriate Metaphor

In order to be effective, the content and the form of the metaphor both must be well-suited to the client. If the client acts restless or bored, the content or the delivery is probably not interesting and absorbing enough. The story must be about a topic that holds the client's interest long enough for the story to be told! While being naturalistic, the delivery of the story must also be sufficiently animated to absorb the client's attention.

The form of the story or anecdote should reflect the process level relationship patterns that characterize the client's current issues without being so blatant and literal as to cause the client unnecessary discomfort or self-consciousness. If the client acts annoyed or uncomfortably asks, ''Why are you telling me this?'' the metaphor may be too direct or adequate rapport may not have yet been achieved, or both.

In either of the above cases, the therapist should alter what he is doing, using the client's ongoing response as a guide. If there are doubts or confusion about the client's reaction, the therapist should simply stop comfortably for a moment and ask the client to describe what he is experiencing. If the client's current experience is unsatisfactory, the therapist can comfortably ask him to consider what he would like to experience instead. The therapist can then use the client's description to appropriately alter the metaphor or to drop the storytelling for the moment.

Emphasizing Therapeutic Messages

Key elements in the story can be indirectly marked out for the client by shifts in the therapist's voice tone, speech rhythm, breathing rate, or body movements. Subtle emphasis can also be created by inserting the client's name at the beginning or end of a meaningful phrase. For example:

> My friend visited a Chinese restaurant called The Dragon, and after dinner we were served fortune cookies. He broke open his fortune cookie, and it said, JERRY (*client's name*) YOU WILL NOW BEGIN TO FIND A SOLUTION TO YOUR PRESENT DIFFICULTIES. My friend laughed heartily at the message. He was surprised when he returned home from his business trip to find that some interesting changes had occurred, and yet he retained his skepticism. He and his wife enjoyed a good laugh about that.

Eliciting an Altered State of Consciousness

Good storytellers have traditionally been described as telling tales that are ''entrancing'' or ''spellbinding.'' Telling a story or anecdote in a context of deep therapeutic rapport will often have the effect of eliciting an altered state of consciousness in the listener, popularly known as a hypnotic trance. Storytelling is an age-old method of inducing a receptive state in which the listener can more readily respond to metaphorical messages.

Telling an absorbing story or anecdote while simultaneously non-verbally pacing the client will generally elicit a hypnotic trance state. This effect can be observed in the client by watching for the following hypnotic phenomena: The client will begin to exhibit a gradual relaxation and flattening of facial muscles; there may be a slight change in facial coloring; a slight shift in breathing patterns, an absence of superficial body movements, dilation of pupils, and in some cases, eyes closing may also be observed. The fact that some clients comfortably close their eyes in response to being told a story is not surprising considering that "bedtime" stories are a time-honored strategy for putting young children to sleep!

Reorientation

Generally a client will spontaneously reorient at the end of a story in response to the changes in tone and rhythms of the storyteller's voice that naturally occur as a story reaches a conclusion. However, this is not always the case. Therefore, it is a good idea for the therapist to work out comfortable strategies for assisting a client in reorienting to a normal waking state. There are several ways to naturalistically accomplish this.

Gently asking the client how she is feeling will generally assist the client in becoming reoriented. The therapist's voice tone and volume should communicate security in relaxation; the client is apt to be in a highly suggestible state following a metaphor and it is important that any implicit suggestions be of a highly positive and comforting nature. Depending on the nature of the therapeutic relationship, a light touch on the hand, arm, or shoulder may also be used as a naturalistic signal to help the client reorient. A more direct method is to invite the client to reorient:

"As you begin to comfortably drift back to your everyday state of awareness, you can bring with you a feeling of comfort and refreshment, as well as any new learnings that are of benefit to you, leaving anything best left unconscious in your unconscious awareness.'' If the client has been in a relatively deep trance the therapist can comfortably wonder aloud: '' . . . I wonder which part of you will begin to wake up first, comfortably, enjoying that fluttering of the eyelids beginning to open, feeling the sensations in fingers, toes, gently waking up all over. . . .'' The therapist should try to gauge the casual ''wondering'' to correspond to the client's movements, for instance mentioning the eyes opening as the client's eyes begin to open.

Another option is for the therapist to establish an understanding with the client prior to telling the metaphor that: ''After I have finished the story, I will say the word, 'Okay (client's name)' and you will return to your everyday state of awareness, refreshed and relaxed.'' At the end of the story, the therapist can pause for a minute or two to allow the client to integrate the messages that have been given and then simply say the word ''okay'' in the same tone in which it was initially delivered.

If the client does not respond to these signals right away, it is likely that she is still engaged in unconscious integrations and needs a little more time. In this case the client can be given suggestions of reassurance that more time is available:

You really do have ALL THE TIME IN THE WORLD IN THE NEXT 5 (10, 15) MINUTES OF CLOCK TIME.

This technique will enable the client to experience a subjective altering of his experience of time, so that his unconscious needs can be met within the time available. It is also sometimes useful to remind a client that:

You can rest assured that you can comfortably return to these experiences at a later time to comfortably complete anything you may have left unfinished. . . .

In assisting a client in comfortably reorienting, it is important that the therapist consistently convey a context of relaxation, acceptance, and security through his voice rhythm and tone as well as the actual words being said. Inevitably the client will reorient; it is important that the therapist realize that each client will have his own idiosyncratic ways of going into and coming out of trance states. These individual differences should be appreciated and respected.

Dynamics of Therapeutic Metaphors Reviewed in Brief

In summary, a metaphorical story should provide a metaphorical representation of the client's current problem state, hope, the actual therapeutic change, and a provision for utilizing predictable backslides to further integrate and enhance the desired therapeutic outcome. While telling the metaphor the therapist should provide the client with a continuous communication of support and acceptance by nonverbally pacing the client. To further ensure rapport, the therapist should "speak the client's language" by using descriptive words that are characteristic of the client's most favored representational system, and employ subjects and themes that reflect the client's interests. Throughout the story, the client's ongoing verbal and nonverbal reactions will serve as the therapist's guide to appropriate style of delivery and content of the stories.

Initially, the above may seem like a lot for the therapist to remember while telling a client a therapeutic metaphor. However, with practice, this technique can become an automatic process that is part of the therapist's personal repertoire. Once learned, the process of effectively telling a metaphor becomes not unlike the spontaneous movements of a dancer or jazz musician. Once a therapist becomes thoroughly familiar with the prerequisites for creating therapeutic metaphors, it is possible to spontaneously generate an appropriate and effective therapeutic metaphor during a therapy session.

THE SPONTANEOUSLY TOLD METAPHOR VS. THE CONSTRUCTED METAPHOR

There are definite advantages both to the preplanned, structurally developed metaphor created ahead of time outside the therapy setting, and the spontaneous metaphor the therapist creates during the therapy session. Admittedly, the metaphor that is designed prior to the therapy session is likely to be more smoothly delivered and elegantly constructed. However, a preplanned story does not allow the therapist as much flexibility in changing and altering the content of the story to meet the client's current mood and ongoing response.

A story that was formulated based on the therapist's impressions of the client during the previous therapy session may not be appropriate for today's session! Furthermore, a previously planned, rehearsed story has a tendency to sound rehearsed, thereby sacrificing some of the absorbing quality of aliveness inherent in a spontaneously told story.

The spontaneously told story, on the other hand, is apt to be based on the therapist's personal life experience and constitutes an immediate and highly personalized response to the needs of the client.

For the purpose of initially learning how to create therapeutic metaphors and further perfecting this skill, it is useful to regularly plan and then write out or tape a series of metaphors outside the therapy situation. However, for actual therapeutic interventions with chronic and resistant clients, the author recommends that therapists learn to spontaneously generate metaphors within the therapy situation. Spontaneously told metaphors have a quality of "aliveness" that is potently effective in meeting the contact needs of the chronic client.

Whether the metaphor is preplanned or spontaneously told, it is the responsibility of the therapist to personalize it to the point that it is no longer merely a technique, but instead constitutes an immediate, meaningful and naturalistic response to the client's needs. When this condition is met, the metaphor will be "irresistible" to the client.

Effectively Telling Spontaneous Metaphors

In order to effectively tell spontaneous therapeutic metaphors in the therapy situation, the therapist must meet the following conditions:

1) The therapist must maintain an ongoing state of deep rapport with the client.

2) The therapist must have an understanding of the prerequisites for an effective metaphor.

3) The therapist must have an accurate understanding of the client's current issues, as well as acceptance and appreciation of the client's personal strengths, resources, debilities, and idiosyncrasies.

4) While telling the metaphor the therapist should remain in a deeply relaxed, highly responsive state of focused alertness. This can be enhanced by the therapist taking a few minutes to employ a favorite relaxation technique prior to each therapy session and allowing herself to clear her mind of extraneous issues.

5) When the above conditions have been met, the therapist can simply "allow" herself to spontaneously tell an effective and appropriate story in response to the client's needs.

CONSIDERATIONS REGARDING THE THERAPIST'S STATE OF AWARENESS

Bandler and Grinder (1979) describe a state in which the therapist is " . . . completely in sensory experience." In this state, the therapist is completely absorbed in the external reality of the client's responses and behavior. The therapist intentionally suspends his own internal reality, "internal feelings, voices, pictures. . . ." This enables the therapist to respond immediately to the client in a highly focused, relaxed and spontaneous fashion. This is an ideal state for enabling the therapist to tell appropriate and effective therapeutic metaphors in a naturalistic, focused, and meaningful fashion (Bandler & Grinder, 1979, p. 55).

A focused, relaxed, externally oriented state is virtually essential for effectively telling spontaneous metaphors. At the same time, it should be understood that the therapist's relaxed, focused state within the treatment session is not a substitute for the therapist spending some time consciously examining the issues and problems the client brings to therapy.

For the purpose of telling appropriate spontaneous metaphors during the therapy session, the therapist should prepare outside the therapy session by spending some time identifying the client's general personality patterns, personal strengths and weaknesses, and setting appropriate and identifiable (measurable) treatment goals.

If possible, the therapist should spend a few minutes before and after each therapy session considering all of the above. During the therapy session itself, however, the author strongly recommends that the therapist simply allow himself to respond to the client and tell meaningful metaphors in the context of a relaxed, focused and attentive state. The resulting level of communication that occurs in this context constitutes the difference between "administering a technique" and naturalistically responding to the client in a spontaneous, fully human, and consequently therapeutically dynamic manner.

Therapy that merely consists of administering a technique risks a level of response that is potentially depersonalizing and alienating to the client. Telling a therapeutic metaphor in a context of deep rapport colored by the therapist's subjective state of relaxation and attentive focus communicates a deep message of integrity that is a hallmark of Ericksonian therapy.

10

Using Metaphors with
Psychotic Clients

The purpose of telling a metaphor to a psychotic client is to naturalistically assist the client in gradually reorienting to a relaxed, comfortable, lucid state. The author's experience in telling metaphors to psychotic clients suggests that stories and anecdotes constitute a valuable resource for reaching and assisting this client population. One of the advantages of metaphors is that they can be told to the client in a nonthreatening manner that facilitates rapport and deepens communication, enabling clients to respond comfortably and at their own pace.

PRACTICAL CONSIDERATIONS FOR
TELLING METAPHORS TO PSYCHOTIC CLIENTS

Psychotic clients tend to be in a highly suggestible trancelike state (Kramer & Brennan, 1964; Zeig, 1974). In order to work effectively with a psychotic client, it is crucial that the therapist maintain a sense of personal relaxation and security. Often the psychotic client will tend to "pick up" and begin to embody whatever emotional feeling state the therapist is projecting nonverbally. This is why a slightly agitated psychotic client usually becomes more agitated if he senses he is beginning to scare or upset the therapist or other clients.

The easiest and most effective way to help a psychotic client feel safe and secure is for the therapist to project that feeling in voice tone and rhythm, body posture, and breathing pattern, while simultaneously pacing the client. Soon the therapist will lead the client into a more secure, relaxed and more adaptive state.

If the therapist is not aware of principles of indirect suggestion (Erickson, 1964b) and nonverbal pacing communication (Bandler & Grinder, 1975), there is the danger of the client inadvertently "leading" the therapist into an agitated or otherwise unsatisfactory state! The therapist then begins to experience some of the client's discomfort and anxiety. The author suspects that many therapists' "burnout" symptoms result from this phenomenon.

Topic Selection

When working with psychotic clients, it is usually best to tell naturalistic, conversational kinds of metaphorical stories and anecdotes. Vivid, real-life stories are apt to be more helpful than abstract, theoretical stories in securing the client's attention and assisting the client in creating a pathway back to lucidity.

Delivering the Metaphor

It is important to remember that the eventual goal with a psychotic client is to gradually and gently enable the client to reorient to a more relaxed, secure, and eventually lucid state. The psychotic client is already in a disoriented state and the last thing that client needs is further disorientation, confusion, or additional anxiety at that time. Ericksonian confusion techniques are NOT suitable for psychotic clients.

If a psychotic client is offered a secure context of acceptance and plenty of time, the client will usually be more than willing to at least temporarily reorient to a more comfortable, relaxed, and nonpsychotic state. Psychotic behavior is quite often a defense against others. Once the client realizes that the context is one of safety, the psychotic behavior stands a good chance of being dropped. As in virtually all therapeutic interactions, the therapist's expectations of positive outcome are crucial; the client will sense the therapist's attitude and respond accordingly.

Case Example
Utilizing a Psychotic Experience Through Metaphor

Nathan was a 27-year-old client with a three-year history of recurrent psychiatric hospitalizations for psychotic depression. He was currently unemployed and living with his parents in much the same fashion as he had before his recent four years of successful employment as a bricklayer. He had lost his job while hospitalized during a recent psychotic episode; his employer had been forced to hire someone else to meet construction deadlines.

Nathan was well-liked by many old friends from his former high school class. He was attractive and personable, with a good sense of humor. Since his psychotic episodes, however, he had made no new friends and saw his old friends infrequently.

He spent his time helping his father on the farm and tinkering with old cars. He talked very little. His parents appeared to have a stable marriage. Nathan's low self-esteem and recurrent depression were a mystery to his family and friends, as well as to the various therapists who had worked with Nathan. He had been receiving treatment over the past four years.

The frequency of Nathan's psychotic episodes had increased slowly but steadily. He was hospitalized following a psychotic episode approximately once every six months. He had been seen extensively for family, individual and group therapy, and had received chemotherapy. He appeared to have a drinking problem and had been referred for alcoholism treatment. However, he had consistently refused such treatment.

Like many chronic clients, Nathan showed up for treatment sporadically, generally requesting to see a therapist only when he was in a near psychotic state, and frequently calling to cancel appointments when he was functioning more comfortably. He had been hospitalized five times in the last two and a half years.

At this point Nathan left the locale of the mental health center with a friend to take a trip to Mexico. Apparently, during the trip, Nathan had begun to feel anxious. His friend had reportedly given him a dose of LSD to "help" him "feel better." Nathan then had the following hallucinated experience about which he continued to obsess, darkly speculating about the "message" it contained:

Nathan had stopped for a break from driving at a truck stop with his friend. Nathan said,

> I was feeling pretty good. I had been kind of nervous but then I took the acid, and now I was watching a sunset and I was feeling okay. We walked into the truck stop and we had some coffee. Then I walked up to one of these machines. You know, the kind that you put a quarter in and your fortune comes out. I put my money in and this is the message that came out: YOUR FUTURE IS YOUR PAST.
>
> I read that message, and that hit me so hard. That is exactly my life. I've been going backwards all my life ever since I was 17 and I'm continuing to go backwards and I know I always will. I don't know what to do. I've been thinking about killing myself. I've taken five more hits of acid (three weeks ago) trying to forget it. My friend says there wasn't any truck stop and there wasn't any message on any machine, but I know there was and it was real and THIS IS HOW MY LIFE IS AND HAS BEEN AND WILL BE.
>
> My mother says that I have to forget this or I'll end up right back in the hospital. And my Dad gets mad and says I need to forget it and start thinking about getting a job and doing other things. I know they're right. My friends come by the house and they say, "Look man, it's over, forget it, relax, it's okay." But I just can't quit thinking about it. It comes back over and over again in my head, the words, "Your future is in your past." It means I'm going backwards. And I don't know how to turn myself around. . . . I just can't stop thinking about it.

The author had been asked to see the client at this point to determine if he should be transferred to an inpatient psychiatric unit, or if the hospitalization could be avoided through outpatient treatment. Nathan had not slept for three nights and had not eaten for two days. He looked terrible. His hair and clothing were unwashed, his eyes looked hollow and dilated. He spoke rapidly and his hands trembled.

Nathan's first psychotic episode had occurred at age 17. A casual conversation was begun in which he related the above description of his recent trip and voiced fears about "always feeling like THIS." He was asked how "this" felt, and he said he felt like he was right now on "acid" even though it had been three weeks since he had taken that or any drug. He was scheduled to see a psychiatrist in a few hours to determine if his anxious sensation could be alleviated by some sort of medication.

During this conversation, the therapist "paced" Nathan's nonverbal responses. This was accomplished by the therapist matching the movements of a finger resting on a desk to the rhythm of Nathan's breathing.

The therapist listened attentively to Nathan's compulsively detailed account of the above story. When Nathan finally fell silent, the therapist observed, looking meaningfully at Nathan, "Drugs always eventually wear off, Nathan." The client paused as if to consider this, and then said, "Just hearing you say that makes me feel a lot safer, just knowing it won't last forever like this. . . . "

The therapist's observation that "drugs always eventually wear off" conveys acceptance of the client's belief that his current sensations were drug-induced. While the fact that he would still be reacting to the drugs after three weeks is improbable, it is a useful belief for the client because it will enable him to accept the premise that he will eventually feel better. The word, "eventually" serves to account for the fact that the client probably will not experience immediate relief. The phrase "always eventually" then constitutes an undeniable reassurance and indirect suggestion that the client is going to eventually feel good again.

Nathan again offered a compulsively detailed account of the experience with the fortune-telling machine. He then described in detail the arguments he had experienced with his friends, parents, and other therapist who all denied that the experience had been "real." Nathan said, "I wish it wasn't real. But it was real, even if I'm the only one who saw or heard those words. They are an exact description of my life, where I'm at . . . now." The therapist responded, "I believe you."

The client visibly relaxed. The therapist then said, "You've been thinking about this a lot, and that makes sense because it obviously is very important. At the same time, even the most hard-working bricklayer (Nathan's profession) takes a lunch break now and then." The client was then offered a glass of water which he accepted. The following dialogue ensued:

Therapist: Do you remember Kate Brown? (*a consulting therapist*)

Client: No.

Therapist: Is your car working yet?

Client: No. I still have some work to do on it.

Therapist: Well, today when you were talking, I found myself remembering a story. . . .

When Kate was 17, she didn't have her own car. Her parents had two cars which was necessary because they lived way up in the country in Black County and it was 15 miles to the nearest town and 20 miles to the nearest high school. Kate was the kind of kid who liked to have a good time but basically behaved herself. . . . Anyway, one weekend, in the middle of her senior year, her parents went away. They left her with one of the cars and gave her the instructions that she could use the car as much as she wanted as long as she obeyed the one following "rule": She could take the car anywhere she wanted, as long as she left at least half a tank of gas in it and there wasn't more than 30 miles on the odometer (*client nods*). Now Kate's father was a pretty smart old "codger"; he had raised six kids before Kate and there were three more younger than Kate in the family. Somehow he had gotten wind that there was a beer party across town at a farmhouse about 16 miles away. He didn't care if Kate went into town, but he was worried about her going to a beer party. And he didn't want to worry Kate's mother by talking directly about it. (*Nathan*

begins to laugh appreciatively; this was similar to the pattern between
his own mother and father.)
Therapist: So what do you think happened after they left?
Client: She stayed home, but she had a bunch of friends over.
Therapist: Close . . . but not exactly (*continuing to pace client*).
Client: (*laughing*) TELL me what happened. (*It is useful to get the client*
curious about a story's outcome.)
Therapist: Okay, you can REST ASSURED, NATHAN, that Kate's
father would have grounded her for at least two weeks if she
had put any extra mileage on that car. So Kate was in a bind.
Being 17 years old, the last thing she wanted was to stay home
on a Friday night. But she was also wanting to avoid getting
into trouble with her parents. And this was hard because 17-
year-olds are always a little rebellious.

#1. (PROBLEM)

Friday night she had two friends over. They watched TV
and they played Monopoly. By 8:30 p.m. they were feeling
kind of UPTIGHT, NOT KNOWING WHAT TO DO TO FEEL
BETTER about how the weekend was going.

#2. (DESIRED STATE—CLIENT'S HOPE)

She knew there was a party going on just 16 miles away.
She could go and she would for sure have a good time, really
ENJOYING herself with her friends. . . .

#3. (OBJECTION)

She could go to the party; but if she did, Kate WOULDN'T
HAVE ENOUGH MILES LEFT on the odometer to go into
town even once during the rest of the weekend. And because
there would be 32 instead of 30 miles on the car, her father
would suspect that she had gone to the beer party in addition
to disobeying about the mileage. Kate had GOTTEN INTO
TROUBLE with her father before and had gotten "grounded"

for two weeks; it had felt like "forever." She even now remembers what a drag that was! Anyway, what do you think she did? (*This serves to gauge the client's level of interest. In addition to observing a client's nonverbal cues of apparent absorption and interest, it is often helpful to directly check to determine reaction to the story.*)

Client: She went away and she got grounded 'cause her old man found out.

Therapist: Yes and no.

Client: What happened? (*appears absorbed and interested*)

Therapist: Well, actually, she went outside the house and just stood there with her two friends. They were already practically bored to tears. . . .

#4. (MOTIVATION TO CHANGE)

. . . And it seemed like the evening was only going to get WORSE; boring beyond their wildest dreams. None of them had access to any other car other than Kate's father's car. They stood there looking at the road, one of those typical dusty country roads. But you know how country roads are . . . (*Nathan lives at the end of a long country lane.*)

. . . They must have stood there 15 minutes and not a single car went by. They stood there for half an hour and not a single car went by. They probably could have stood there an hour and not a single car went by! (*Nathan laughs.*)

Client: Were they trying to hitchhike?

Therapist: I don't think that occurred to them. But even if it did, "fat chance" on a country road.

Client: (*laughing again*) Yeah—fat chance! (*pause*) So . . . what happened? Did they do some drugs? (*This is a sign that the client is beginning to identify with the story.*)

Therapist: (*with mock incredulity*) On a country road, in 1968, in Black County?!

Client: I see what you mean . . . fat chance! (*laughs*)

Therapist: So they just stood there for a while, just doing nothing. Finally a strange car turned into the driveway. This scared them a little because it wasn't anyone they knew. But it just turned out to be somebody lost, turning around; the driver asked for directions back into town.

#5. (RESOURCE)

Watching that car backing out of the driveway, an IDEA hit Kate. (*The therapist lowers voice conspiratorily; this is a foreshadowing of the story's deeper message.*) Then the three girls climbed into Kate's father's car. What do you think they did?

Client: (*laughing*) They went to the party—she disobeyed her old man, and later she got grounded. . . .

Therapist: Well, actually, she obeyed the old man, AND she did go to the party.

The client does not speak; his eyes are riveted on the therapist; breathing is relaxed. He appears deeply absorbed, listening attentively.

#6. (CHANGE)

Therapist: They got in the car and they backed out the driveway, and then, Nathan, YOU KNOW COUNTRY ROADS, SO YOU KNOW THAT YOU CAN CAREFULLY AND VERY COMFORTABLY GO PRETTY FAR BACKWARDS WHILE GOING IN THE ACTUAL DIRECTION IN WHICH YOU REALLY WANT AND NEED TO GO FORWARD. On a country road, you can drive carefully and go pretty far often without meeting another car. So they back up and they keep going backwards with one eye on the rearview mirror and the radio playing FAVORITE TUNES. (*The reference to "carefully" and "comfortably" and the allusion to "favorite tunes" all serve to indirectly suggest a relaxed and positive context.*)

(*The client smiles slightly, his hand tremors have ceased and his breathing is even and relaxed. His eyes look straight ahead and he appears to be in a light trance state.*)

Therapist: After about half an hour of slow but safe driving THEY ARRIVED HAPPILY AT THE PARTY. THEY HAD BACKED UP ALL THE WAY THERE!

(*The client's smile broadens, lips twitch, and he laughs softly.*)

Therapist: They each drank a beer, had a great time, and then carefully BACKED BACK home. (*Client smiles again.*) On the way home, they started to joke about where else they could back up to that weekend.

(*Client continues to appear deeply absorbed.*)

Therapist: They realized that (*meaningful look at client*), YOU CAN TRAVEL BACKWARDS TO ANYPLACE YOU WANT TO GO FORWARDS TO. . . . People on trains DO THAT all the time, COMFORTABLY, WITHOUT REALLY HAVING TO THINK ABOUT IT . . . whenever they happen to sit facing one another and one of them is sitting backwards, facing away from the direction of the desired destination.

(*The client appears deep in thought, seems to be considering the messages of the story.*)

The therapist pauses here. The above communication constitutes a reorientation of the meanings the client has previously attached to going backwards, giving the client the opportunity to use this orientation to take him "anyplace you want to go forwards to." The possibility of conscious interference is provided for by suggesting that the client "do that . . . comfortably, without really having to think about it." In this way, a comfortable context is assured through indirect implication, and the client is given the opportunity to consciously forget the experience following the story if that will best serve his therapeutic needs. The invitation to forget is implied in the words, "without really having to think about it." Since the client is facing the therapist and has described a feeling of going backwards, the reference to people on trains is an indirect reference to the client and therapist and contains a reframing message to the client regarding the result of going backwards.

#7. (FUTURE INTEGRATION)

Therapist: The next night Kate felt bored again and she thought about going out. She had already backed out of the driveway, when she stopped for a moment and said to herself, "NOW THAT YOU'VE ALREADY GONE BACKWARDS AGAIN YOU HAVE A CHOICE." She had saved up enough miles on the odometer going backwards the night before so that she could GO FORWARD into town COMFORTABLY for a movie or something else that she wanted WITH NO NEED TO BACK UP UNNECESSARILY. When her father came home, she told him the whole story—it was too funny not to tell him. And he began to laugh. He thought it was very funny and she did not get into any trouble with him. I suppose nowadays a father might be more worried, but especially back then, there was so little traffic on the country roads. Years later, Kate and her father still laugh about it . . . (*pause*).

Client: (*quietly, thoughtfully*) She found the EASY WAY. (*looks questioningly at therapist*)

Therapist: (*meaningfully*) THAT'S RIGHT.

Client: And her father wasn't mad—no one got . . . mad?

Therapist: Right.

Client: . . . I forget what we're talking about . . .

Therapist: (*comfortably*) That's okay with me; is it okay with you?

Client: Yeah, it's fine . . . (*reorienting, beginning to move about in chair and glance comfortably around the room, appears relaxed, a slight smile on face*) I feel like I just went to a party . . . like what you were telling me . . . (*pause*).

Therapist: Is that a good feeling?

Client: Yeah, it's a good feeling . . . but I'm awfully tired.

The client then mentioned again that he had not slept for the past three nights and had not been sleeping very well for several nights previously. He said he was very much looking forward to going home and going to sleep. Transportation home was arranged and he went home and did just that.

When Nathan did not show up for a scheduled appointment with the psychiatrist the next day, inquiry was made. His mother disclosed that he had slept through the night and for most of the next day. He had then eaten some food and bathed. He appeared oriented and was lucid when he showed up for a therapy appointment the next day. He made no reference to his previous "going backwards" obsession.

The following day, Nathan announced his plans to admit himself to the local drug and alcohol abuse unit. He was admitted and later discharged. He has maintained his sobriety for nearly three years to date with only two short slipups; no further hospitalizations have been required. To date the client has made no further mention of his "going backwards" obsession and has maintained a level of orientation and lucidity that allows him to comfortably live in the community.

Recent inquiry disclosed that Nathan is now employed part-time as a drug abuse counselor, is planning to move into his own apartment, has made some new friends, and is enjoying a social life.

POST-METAPHOR FOLLOW-UP WITH FORMERLY PSYCHOTIC CLIENTS

When working with clients who have been described as resistant or have a history of chronicity, follow-up is important. Many chronic clients regress to previous symptomatic behavior in an apparent attempt to get needed support from the therapist and the treatment community.

When some form of ongoing contact with the therapist or the therapeutic community is provided, regression is less likely to occur. The follow-up can take the form of written inquiries or phone calls from the therapist, community support groups, attendance in partial day hospitalization programs, or simply an understanding that the client can arrange to see the therapist if needed. Erickson did informal follow-up when he saw his client in the community at a "casual social gathering."

Reassurance of the therapist's continuing concern and good wishes can be conveyed in just a few words, and yet this simple gesture seems to have a powerful effect in reassuring the client that he will not be "penalized" for becoming lucid and asymptomatic!

Nathan continues to see a therapist and attends a day hospital program sporadically, on an "as needed" basis. He has an understanding with his current therapist that he can schedule a time "just to talk," and can reenter the local day treatment program for a few days for some support if he is feeling low. The author now lives in a distant state, and Nathan has telephoned approximately once a year for the past three years, "just to let you know how things are going."

11

Changing Chronic Problem Behaviors into Therapeutic Resources

Erickson: There was a patient standing around the ward for six or seven years. He didn't talk. He'd go to the cafeteria . . . go to bed when told, go to the bathroom . . . but for the most part he stood.

You could talk to him by the hour without getting a response. One day I made certain he would make a response . . . I took one of those floor polishers over to him, wrapped his fingers around the handle. He stood there. Every day I'd tell him, "Move that floor polisher."

So he began moving it an inch back and forth. Each day I would increase the length that he would push the floor polisher, until I had him going clear around the ward . . . and he began talking. He began accusing me of abusing him by making him polish the floor all day long. I told him, "If you want to do something else, I'm perfectly willing." And so he began making beds. And he began talking, giving his history, expressing his delusions. And pretty soon I was able to give him ground privileges. And within a year he was able to go home and work . . . He was still psychotic but he could adjust to the outside world. (Rosen, 1982, pp. 199–200)

Within the context of most problematic behavior exists a pattern or a personality resource that can be therapeutically utilized to lead to less constricting, more "normal" socially acceptable choices for the client. This chapter will provide specific guidelines for utilizing chronic problematic behaviors. Case examples are provided to illustrate techniques for achieving rapport and intervening in the behavior of a chronically violent client, creating therapeutic alternatives for a chronic runaway client, and utilizing the existing responses of a severely withdrawn client.

LONG-TERM BEHAVIOR PROBLEMS

In dealing with a long-term problematic behavior, the therapist is likely to be initially unsure how to effectively utilize the existing behavior to lead to therapeutic change. While other details of the intervention are dictated by the nature of the behavior and of idiosyncrasies of the client, the first step of the intervention is always the same: *Achieve rapport with the client!* This can be accomplished by directly talking with the client or can be accomplished indirectly through symbolic nonverbal communication, stories and anecdotes, or messages arranged to be communicated to the client through individuals other than the therapist.

Indirect symbolic nonverbal communication can take a variety of forms depending on the creativity, flexibility and personal style of the therapist. The most basic form of nonverbal behavioral communication simply requires that the therapist join the client in doing what the client is already doing.

Utilizing an Occupational Therapy Activity with
Symbolic Nonverbal Communication

In a hospital or day treatment setting, the therapist can communicate acceptance and support naturalistically by joining the client in an occupational therapy activity such as cooking or crafts. If the client performs poorly at these tasks, it may be helpful in achieving rapport with the client for the therapist to join the client in "failing" in some way or at least demonstrating uncertainty about the sequence of the occupational therapy task.

If the client tends to get mocked or criticized by other clients while engaged in occupational therapy tasks, it may be useful for the therapist to arrange for the occupational therapy staff or other staff to come in and criticize the therapist!

A therapist who habitually made poor omelets achieved rapport with a chronic client by joining that client at a cooking activity. The client, who was also an unskilled cook, joined the therapist in cooking a nearly inedible meal! Later, the client and therapist shared the humorous ribbing and "blame" they received from the staff and clients about the "awful" meal. Previously, the client had refused to talk about himself or his difficulties.

After the cooking experience, the client was able to talk to the therapist intimately, with the eventual result that the therapist achieved a successful therapeutic intervention. Years later, the client still wrote occasionally to the therapist and made humorous but meaningful allusions to "the time we cooked breakfast together."

The author, a notoriously clumsy volleyball player, successfully utilized this debility by joining a client volleyball team and requesting "coaching" from various previously resistant clients. By joining the client as a peer and demonstrating that she also had debilities and vulnerabilities, the author secured rapport with the clients. In some cases, in order to make the client feel safe and adequate enough to achieve therapeutic rapport, it may be necessary for the therapist to enter into a situation where the client can outperform the therapist, as in this volleyball example.

The therapist's willingness to truly join with a client on a symbolic behavioral level, either metaphorically or actually joining the client in what the client is already doing, can have a powerful effect on enabling clients to overcome fear and other forms of "resistance."

In joining the client volleyball team in order to achieve rapport with "resistant" clients, the author did not initially realize the degree to which this activity would change the client's perceptions of her.

Following several weeks of volleyball activities, a number of previously belligerent, acting-out, day hospital clients became congenial when in the author's presence, giving her the benefit of social behavior reserved for peers and friends.

As the director of the hospital program, the author functioned as the limit setter for many of the clients who exhibited abusive and acting-out behavior. Following the volleyball experience, a group of the clients who had previously been, at best, noncompliant and "difficult" joined together to make the author a hilarious volleyball "cheerleader" costume to wear to a volleyball competition with another treatment program!

The clients told the author, with obvious sincerity, "You really are a terrible volleyball player. We're helping you get better at volleyball . . . you really need it! And you're helping us." The relationship had become one of peers, yet with decidedly different roles. Aware of the role of demoralization in chronic clients and the staff who work with them, the author enjoyed being perceived as a "cheerleader" by the clients.

In joining the client in an occupational therapy activity, it is important that the therapist's demonstration of lack of skill be real and not a phony attempt! The experienced chronic client or other client who has been in therapy long enough to get labeled "resistant" is likely to be quick to sense any dishonesty on the part of the therapist.

If the therapist's behavior appears contrived or phony, the attempt to achieve rapport will merely result in the client feeling patronized. Therefore, the therapist should arrange to join the client in an activity which in reality is at least as difficult for the therapist as for the client.

Therapists seeing clients individually can easily adapt the above naturalistic strategies to everyday activities. Erickson treated a chronic psychiatric client in the context of watching television together once a week in Erickson's living room!

In the case of a delusional client, sometimes more extreme expressions of rapport are necessary. For example, in order to secure rapport with a delusional paranoid client, Erickson joined the client in wrapping string around the bars of the room to assist the client in creating protection (see chapter 2, p. 10).

Other forms of nonverbal behavioral communication include the therapist acting out a behavior that is a symbolic metaphorical representation of what the client is doing. Erickson once put his coat on backwards in order to achieve rapport with a psychotic client who was behaving and talking in a bizarre manner. Erickson's symbolic nonverbal behavior effectively matched that of the client, thereby communicating acceptance and support.

Carl Whitaker refers to a strategy in which the therapist goes to sleep during a presumably inactive therapy session with a schizophrenic client in order to symbolically communicate a feeling of safety and "reduce the terror" of the client (Whitaker, 1982). Viewed as metaphorical communication, the therapist's behavior of going to sleep tells the client that there is nothing to fear, that the therapist obviously trusts and accepts the client.

Other indirect nonverbal strategies include the therapist moving progressively closer to the client over a period of days or weeks until the client becomes comfortable with the therapist standing at a conversational distance; communicating support and acceptance through a warm tone; smiling directly toward one client while speaking comfortably with another client, and basically any form of nonthreatening behavior on the part of the therapist that serves to convey acceptance and support to clients.

The therapist can also use anecdotes and stories as a way to achieve rapport with the client by sending a metaphorical message of support and acceptance. For example, the therapist can tell the client stories about positive relationships the therapist has experienced with individuals who in some way indirectly resemble the client. Or the therapist can tell a metaphor in which two individuals, one indirectly representing the client and one indirectly representing the therapist, enjoyed a positive and rewarding relationship: "You may have heard the story of the country mouse coming to visit the city mouse and the city mouse coming to visit the country mouse . . . ," etc.

If the client reacts to the metaphor with suspicion or paranoia, it is an indication that the metaphor is too directly representative of the client and that a less direct and less threatening approach is needed.

When working with a chronic or "resistant" client, it is safe to assume that much patience will be required on the part of the therapist. Chronic clients not infrequently "test" their therapists to determine if the support and acceptance conveyed are real. This is not to imply that chronic and resistant clients intentionally and consciously set out to reject their therapists' attempts to join them. Rather, chronic clients by their nature require a high degree of acceptance and support in order to risk a relationship in what to them is often a frightening and dangerous world.

Case Example
Alice: Utilizing the Behavior of a Chronically Violent Client*

One of the primary difficulties facing the therapist who works with a chronically aggressive, belligerent, or threatening client is that success will often be in proportion to the therapist's willingness to become closely involved with the client. This is difficult because the client's aggressive behavior serves as a well-practiced and powerful means of keeping others at arm's length. Such was the case with the following client:

Alice was a 25-year-old client who had a four-year history of violent, acting-out behavior in the community, with repeated arrests, suicide attempts, and cyclical hospitalizations following her physical outbursts. Typically, Alice formed romantic liaisons with rough, alcoholic men who cheated on her. She characteristically attempted to surprise her boyfriend and the woman he was cheating with at one of the local bars where she attempted to beat them up. Although Alice was petite, she was a skilled streetfighter and usual-

---

*This case example is taken from a paper written by the author for the Second International Congress on Ericksonian Approaches to Psychotherapy and Hypnotherapy held in Phoenix, Arizona, 1983, and published in Vol. II of the Proceedings, *Ericksonian Psychotherapy: Clinical Applications* (Brunner/Mazel, 1985).

ly delivered several respectable blows before the police came to take her away.

Alice was referred to the psychiatric day hospital program through a court order. For the first three months she spoke rarely, sulking angrily around the program premises, snarling that she was technically in compliance with the court order. The author's direct attempts to make contact with her served only to elicit anger and threatening behavior.

For two months, the author spoke little to Alice but progressively moved in closer and closer, beginning from across the room and eventually achieving a conversational distance of a few feet without eliciting anger or threats. However, any direct expression of support or interest elicited an angry or suspicious response.

The staff arranged to make "random" positive observations about Alice's improved appearance, behavior with peers, skills at crafts, etc., deliberately intended to be overheard by Alice or other clients who would be likely to repeat back to Alice what they had heard being said about her. Any marginally positive behavior was framed in a positive light. After six months of overheard comments, Alice began to seek the staff out.

Alice refused to speak directly about her difficulties. However, she talked willingly about her craft and needlework projects which she worked on daily in the program. The staff responded by telling the client (concerning the needlework projects) "This is good . . . and YOU REALLY CAN FIND A WAY TO USE ALL YOUR ABILITIES IN A WAY THAT LETS YOU WIN." (An avid card player, Alice was a sore loser and an excellent winner.) Alice's characteristic reaction to this comment was, "You're nuts!" However, she began to smile more frequently and her behavior continued to become more gentle and sociable. Suggestions for self-esteem and security were also interspersed in comments to other clients, made with meaningful looks at Alice. The staff wondered, however, if these messages were actually reaching her.

After six months of treatment in the day hospital, Alice was in desperate need of a job; she was sleeping in her car and had little to eat. No one would hire her. One day she came very late to the program and announced triumphantly, "I found a way to use my abilities!'' She had gotten a job as a bouncer in one of the rough local bars. Her previous reputation for erratic and violent behavior served her well. When she asked customers to leave, they left quietly despite her diminutive stature.

Within a year, Alice had progressed from bouncer to barmaid to bartender, and had begun to dress appropriately and attractively. No further violent outbursts or suicide attempts have occurred. Three years later, the client still maintains contact with the author. Alice reports that she is currently completing a college degree in psychology, has enjoyed a rewarding and stable relationship with a man for the past year, and is employed as a secretary.

In repeatedly suggesting that Alice could find rewarding ways to use ALL her abilities, the staff could not have predicted how Alice would find a way to productively use former violent streetfighting behavior. Even the most problematic behavior can often be utilized as a therapeutic resource.

Problematic behavior often contains a behavioral pattern that can be utilized to lead to new and positive changes for the client. That valuable aspect of the existing behavior can be identified by asking the questions below.

1) *What are the client's past and current (a) skills and (b) resources?* Note: List all skills and resources no matter how apparently insignificant they may appear at first glance. One of the hallmarks of Erickson's work was the ability to therapeutically utilize previously overlooked resources. The category of resources includes positive or motivating relationships, the client's immediate environment and community such as existing educational and social opportunities, positive and motivational experiences contained in developmental, social and work history.

2) *What is the pattern of existing problem behavior?*

3) *In what naturalistic context would the existing behavior or some portion of the existing behavior constitute a more adaptive, potentially rewarding and socially acceptable response?* Clues can be derived by considering that all problematic behavior is derived from some exaggeration of everyday human behavior.

The following case example will illustrate the above assessments.

Case Example
Dana: Utilizing Chronic Running-Away Behavior

Dana was a 23-year-old mildly retarded woman who repeatedly ran away whenever she felt overwhelmed by emotions of anger, sadness, or emotional closeness, which she experienced as vulnerability. If restrained from running away, she lashed out violently and desperately at people and objects within reach. Following these episodes, she attempted to slash her wrists and had a history of self-mutilation evidenced by slash and burn marks up and down her arms self-inflicted with razor blades and cigarette lighters.

Dana was referred to a day hospital program as a condition for being accepted at a group home. A neglected and physically abused child, Dana had been removed from her parents' home six years previously. Her acting out and runaway behavior had resulted in a long series of foster home, nursing home and group home placements.

Receiving mental health services for the past six years, Dana's yearly psychiatric inpatient hospitalizations inevitably occurred when her foster placement families or group home staff were at the "end of their rope" in dealing with her episodic violent, withdrawn and runaway behaviors. Efforts at family therapy, behavioral therapy and chemotherapy regimes had been unsuccessful in producing a change in Dana's problem behavior.

When asked by the author what she experienced before, during and after the episodes following her impulse to run away, the client stated:

> I felt so mad. And I felt scared. I felt something coming on like it wasn't me, like I couldn't control it; I couldn't stop myself. Like the devil got into me. And then afterwards I feel so bad, I want to kill myself. I hate myself for the way I act. I don't want to see anybody, I just want to die. I'm just no good. Everybody hates me. Nobody likes me. I hate myself.

Skills and Abilities

Dana was a muscular, athletic appearing woman who evidenced good coordination in physical games. She was an excellent volleyball player. It was learned that in school she had enjoyed long distance running, practicing more than was necessary and enjoying the recognition of her peers.

Two years previously Dana had successfully worked in a nursing home as a cook's helper. She had an ability to follow directions accurately and had successfully learned her way around the nursing home facility, which was a reasonably large building. She had quickly learned directions to and from various points of interest in the small town where she had recently moved to live in the group home.

When not distraught, Dana could carry on a reasonable conversation.

Other Resources

Appearance. Although often sloppily dressed and 20 pounds overweight, Dana had attractive facial features and carried her weight well.

Relationships. Dana described two close female friends who lived in the community, had known her for several years, and had loyally stood by her despite her moodiness and frequent hospitalizations. Occasionally these two friends came to visit Dana wherever she happened to be staying. One or the other of them would take her out to lunch and shopping every few weeks. The two friends had often told Dana that they looked forward to the time when she would live closer to where they lived and would be free to do more things with them. Since Dana shared this same desire, her relationship with the friends functioned as a motivational resource.

Dana also had a memory of a foster family she had truly loved and who had loved her. While her behavior had caused her to be removed from the foster home, she still maintained positive contact with this family who remained supportive and occasionally invited her to come for dinner, although they were clear with her that a future return to the previous living situation was not feasible. The family's ongoing encouragement was a resource.

The fact that acting-out behavior had once resulted in her losing a previous living situation she had valued constituted a further motivational resource to help Dana find another way of expressing herself.

Environment. The group home setting where Dana now lived constituted a further resource. The other residents were Dana's age and generally friendly. The group home staff was supportive and flexible, and took a real interest in Dana.

Community. A local mental health volunteer had offered to give haircuts and grooming lessons to interested people. A community support group was also available to Dana. The local social services department provided Dana with a caseworker to assist in management of Dana's monthly income which consisted of social security benefits.

Dana was a member of a local church which she attended regularly. It was obvious that she willingly maintained her commitments and agreements; to this degree she evidenced an ability to be self-responsible.

Pattern of Problem Behavior

The pattern sequence of Dana's problematic behavior was identified as: feeling overwhelmed, wanting to run away, striking out at other people and objects in the environment, striking out physically at herself, becoming despondent and withdrawn.

Naturalistic Context: Jogging

The impulse to run was identified as being a potentially adaptive and socially acceptable way for the client to let off emotional "steam" if performed in the naturalistic context of choosing to go jogging and then returning to take a shower and put on clean clothing.

Inevitably one of Dana's characteristic episodes of feeling over-whelmed and wanting to run away occurred in the day hospital pro-gram. The immediate intervention was accomplished in the following manner:

Dana had become overwhelmed by feelings of sadness in re-sponse to something said by another client. Since she assumed that she would be somehow physically restrained if she attempted to run away from the premises (in other settings she had in fact been physically restrained), Dana began to voice her impulse to strike out physically.

The therapist was able to avert Dana's violent, acting-out behav-ior by securing rapport and trust through nonverbal communica-tion. Specifically, the therapist maintained a calm, relaxed body posture and tone of voice, meanwhile lightly tapping her fingers on her lap in a rhythm that simulated Dana's larger body move-ments. This had the effect of sending her the message that the therapist was truly "with" her. Dana responded by stopping her rapid movements and threatening behavior long enough for the following discussion to occur:

Therapist: How are you feeling right now, Dana?
Dana: I hate it here! I hate my life! I hate everybody in this room!
   I want to run away . . . I'm going to run away! I'm going to
   leave here! . . . You can't stop me! Don't try or I'll hit you!

At this point the client began to sob and slowly pace back and forth across the room. The therapist approached Dana at a distance and asked her if there was anything she wanted. Dana turned and screamed in apparent exasperation, "Yes, there's something I'm wanting! I'm wanting to get out of this f—ing place!" The therapist asked, "Anything else?"

Dana: Yes! I want you to leave me alone!
Therapist (*approximating the rhythm although not the tone of client's voice*): That seems like a pretty reasonable request! (*shifting to a more intimate conspiratory tone of voice*) The problem I'm having right now, Dana, is that I'm legally responsible for you during

the hours of this program and I'm not sure how to explain your absence to your case manager. (*This was in fact true. The case manager could be expected to take the therapist to task for failing to properly "manage" the client.*)

Client: (*in a tone of voice that approached the therapist's tone*) Tough shit.

Therapist: That's right. It is tough shit. Tough for both of us. What are we going to do? (*the therapist's referential shift to "we" serves to indirectly invite the client to participate in the search for a solution.*)

Client: (*softer tone of voice*) I don't know what you're going to do; but I'm going to leave; I'm going to run (away).

Therapist: (*continuing to match voice rhythm with client's*) Well, I happen to agree with you, Dana; that seems to be just what you need to do right now or it wouldn't feel so important to you. I also agree with your need to run. In fact, I think it is an excellent and healthy way of letting out feelings. (*slight pause*) Not to change the subject . . . but do you jog, Dana?

Dana: (*quietly, looking slightly confused*) No.

Therapist: (*respectful, matter-of-fact tone*) Well, since you want to "run," jogging might be a logical sport for you to try, an enjoyable way for you to get away from here for awhile. I know you really want to do that.

(The context of jogging served to at least temporarily alter the meaning therapist and client were attaching to the word "run." The words "for awhile" served as a qualifier, implying that the client would return to the premises after jogging. The last part of the therapist's communication served to continue to acknowledge that the client wanted to leave.)

Dana: (*laughing*) I think I will.

Therapist: Greg and Terry are going running down Bayou Road in a few minutes; you probably could go with them if you like.

Dana: I'll go run but not with them. I'll run along Bayou Road by MYSELF.

Therapist: I'm not sure you'll have time to jog and take a shower before lunch. What we could do is save you some lunch. There are extra towels in the women's bathroom if you need them.

Dana: I'm not going to eat lunch. I'll see you after I jog.

Dana went jogging, later returned and showered. Going "running'' or jogging subsequently became a resource for her to let off steam when she was feeling overwhelmed or upset. There have been no further incidents of runaway episodes or violent behavior. The next therapeutic task, of course, would be to assist the client in learning to deal more comfortably and directly with the kinds of experiences that sometimes overwhelm her.

Discussion

When working with a client like Dana it is sometimes important to allow the client to keep a portion of her "resistance." In this way the client's need to object can be focused on some small, insignificant variable rather than on the whole therapeutic relationship. Therapists can intentionally provide some inconsequential details within direct suggestions. This serves to provide the client with the opportunity to simultaneously fulfill a need to argue, which may be for some reason necessary to the client, while actually cooperating in the therapeutic endeavor.

In this case, the desired behavioral goal was to enable Dana to take care of her need to physically leave the room for awhile without actually leaving permanently. Contained in the directive to go jogging were the variables of whom she could run with, when, and where. Dana could reject the therapist's suggestions regarding these variables (whom to run with, where to go, whether to leave now or later) without rejecting the general idea of going jogging.

The meaning of leaving was shifted from running away to running to jogging; the advantage of shifting that meaning was the implication that she would return afterwards, refreshed and relaxed. Jogging is not a behavior, even for marathoners, that a person does indefinitely without stopping! The implied expectation is that the jogger returns to the point of departure or some agreed upon point, and traditionally enjoys a shower and some form of cooling liquid refreshment.

Returning to the premises was built into the meaning Dana attached to "jogging." Therefore, by agreeing to jog, Dana had tacitly agreed to return to the program premises. To further reinforce this, the therapist observed, "I'm not sure you have time to jog and take a shower before lunch." Again Dana was given the opportunity to further object and resist some details (whether she took a shower, whether she ate lunch, whether she used the towels). By the use of a series of indirect techniques, the symptomatic behavior was utilized to lead to the more desirable, adaptive and socially acceptable behavior of going for a jog.

Thus far this chapter has illustrated the importance of achieving rapport with the client, identifying the pattern of the client's problematic behavior, and listing the client's skills and resources. In working with some individuals, particularly a severely withdrawn client, the therapist may find that the "resistance" to the therapeutic endeavor may in fact be one of the client's most potent therapeutic resources. The following case example will illustrate how a client's objection to treatment can be utilized therapeutically.

Case Example
Carl: Utilizing the Responses of a Severely Withdrawn Client

Carl was a 35-year-old man who had been repeatedly hospitalized because of episodes in which he refused to eat, drink, bathe, or speak for days. When pushed by his family and therapists, he became physically violent. Previous attempts at group and individual therapy had been unsuccessful because Carl refused to speak. The client gave no evidence of being delusional and appeared intelligent. Previous to the onset of his withdrawn behavior, Carl had earned a college degree. Little else was known about his past life experiences, skills, and abilities.

Asked what he thought would make his life better, Carl stated emphatically, "I want to be left alone!" Rapport was achieved by the therapist offering to assist Carl in his stated goal of getting his family and service providers to leave him alone. Since Carl had been repeatedly hospitalized over a three-year period, he was receiving services from virtually every human service agency in town. The client was asked how each service provider and family member specifically bothered him and what he thought it would take to get them to leave him alone. Carl was uncertain. He reluctantly agreed to attend one of his own treatment staffings to get a more accurate idea of what specifically it would take to get all those people to leave him alone.

Carl's previous treatment decisions had been made either in his absence or with him present as a passive, withdrawn observer. In this treatment staffing, he reluctantly became the active, central participant. With the therapist's support, Carl gradually found out from his parents and each of his service providers what change in his behavior he could use to "manipulate" them into leaving him alone.

The parents' and service providers' descriptions of behaviors that would allow them to leave Carl alone were listed on a piece of paper. The therapist then assisted Carl in negotiating some of the stated details with his parents and the other service providers. This agreement was then written up as a contract and signed by Carl, his family and the service providers. All agreed to meet once a month to assess how the arrangement was working out and to negotiate changes in the contract.

Initially, Carl agreed to bathe, eat, and attend the day hospital program in return for his parents not nagging him and the various social service and mental health workers leaving him alone. Later, the agreement evolved into Carl living independently in his own apartment and getting job training while no longer needing to attend the day hospital program. He became more expressive and outgoing with his peers, and requested individual therapy which he utilized well. The treatment staffings were held every six to eight weeks and eventually comprised Carl's only continuing form of psychotherapy while he continued to function independently in the community.

After two-and-a-half years, only two service providers continued to be involved in Carl's case. When one of them abruptly stopped attending the meetings, Carl almost immediately regressed to his former withdrawn symptomatic behavior. However, he did not regress to the point of requiring inpatient hospitalizations. Instead he chose to return to the day hospital program and continued to live in the community.

Discussion

The author believes that an error was made in Carl's case by the service provider leaving abruptly without giving the client time to adjust to this news. This may have been viewed as a rejection by the client. Additionally, efforts should have been made to ensure that the client had some form of continuing support and contact in the context of his nonsymptomatic "healthy" behavior. Eventually these needs could then be met by the client's family and social peers.

Follow-up of some sort is useful in avoiding the risk of former clients feeling abandoned by the therapist who is seen less and less as the client no longer exhibits the symptomatic behavior. Some clients like Carl may regress as a way to maintain contact and continue to get needed support from the therapeutic community.

The follow-up can take the form of a support group, a peer network of former clients, follow-up appointments, occasional phone calls or letters from the therapist, or other suitable alternatives. Milton Erickson frequently made personal follow-up inquiries at casual social gatherings.

12

Ericksonian Utilization
in Group Settings

Erickson: I had two Jesus Christs on the ward. And they spent the entire day explaining, "I am Jesus Christ." They buttonholed everybody and explained, "I am the real Jesus Christ."

And so I put John and Alberto on a bench and told them, "You sit there. Now each of you tells me you're Jesus Christ. Now John, I want you to explain to Alberto that YOU, not he, is Jesus Christ. Alberto, you tell John, YOU are the real Jesus Christ and that he is not; you are." I kept them sitting on that bench explaining to each other all day long that each was the true Jesus Christ. And after about a month, John said, "I'm Jesus Christ and that crazy Alberto says that he is Jesus Christ." I said to John, "You know John, you say the same thing that he says. And he says the same things that you say. Now I think that one of you is crazy because there is only one Jesus Christ."

John thought that over for a week. He said, "I'm saying the same things that crazy fool is saying. He's crazy and I'm saying what he says. That must mean I'm crazy too; and I don't want to be crazy." (Rosen, 1982, p. 201)

THE GROUP SETTING AS RESOURCE

A valuable experiential learning context for both the therapist and the client, the group setting provides a richly varied, continually changing spectrum of available therapeutic resources. This chapter will offer specific guidelines and suggestions for employing Ericksonian utilization with "chronic" and "resistant" clients in group and milieu group therapy settings. Clinical examples are provided for illustration.

General Considerations

All of the utilization techniques described in previous chapters can generally be applied to group settings. Additionally there are specific techniques ideally suited for group adaptations.

In gearing Ericksonian utilization strategies to group settings, it is useful to assume that all interactions will be heard by all group members and will presumably have various individual therapeutic meanings and values attached by individual group members. For example, if the therapist is listening to self-disclosing observations from one client and realizes that the message being communicated will have therapeutic value for another client, the therapist can indirectly emphasize the message by looking meaningfully at the appropriate other client or gesturing subtly with a finger or body posture in the direction of the unspecified but intended client. Similarly, the therapist can simultaneously address several clients by giving meaningful looks toward intended recipients of specific communications.

ESTABLISHING A CONTEXT OF COMFORT AND SECURITY AS A THERAPEUTIC RESOURCE IN GROUP SETTINGS

As in individual therapy, establishing a context of security and comfort in the group setting is of particular value. This context of comfort and security is then available as a resource for both individuals and for the group as a whole throughout the therapeutic endeavor. The best time to establish this context is initially, at the beginning of the group. The therapist should spend a few minutes prior to the group attending to any unfinished emotional business of his own and establishing his own feeling of comfort and security. The therapist's body posture and other nonverbal communication should communicate an attitude of relaxed, focused, respectful attention.

The therapist's nonverbal communication will immediately begin to establish a context of security in the clients. Long-term psychiatric clients, particularly semi-psychotic or psychotic clients, tend to be in a highly suggestible state and are very responsive to nonverbal communication.

There are a variety of ways to elicit an experience of comfort and security to serve as a context for the group. One indirect strategy is for the therapist to begin group by telling a short anecdote or metaphor that communicates a feeling of comfort and security. Suggestions for relaxation and security can be emphasized through the therapist's tone, facial expression, and other nonverbal communication, as well as by the content of the story. (See Chapter 6 for further guidelines for developing therapeutic metaphors.)

In some settings, the context of comfort and security can then be enhanced by the therapist directing the group to:

> Take a moment or two now BEFORE group begins to adjust your body to the most comfortable position you can find. Keep your eyes open until you recall a pleasant memory of a place you have been and would like to be right now. (*pause*) Now take a moment with eyes opened or closed, whichever is more comfortable, to really enjoy that experience, noticing how your breathing relaxes, deepens, your body becomes comfortably a little warmer or cooler, while at the same time you really notice the comfortable sights and sounds that go with that feeling. You really can bring that comfortable feeling, relaxed and secure, back with you as you begin to participate in group today, comfortably looking around the room, enjoying that feeling throughout the day, recalling that feeling of comfort and security, knowing it is there inside you whenever you need it.

The therapist can then (optionally) invite the clients to begin group by describing their own symbols for a relaxed, secure state. This will in turn further enhance a relaxed, comfortable state in other group members. If some form of the above exercise is done daily prior to the group beginning, group members will soon attach a context of security and comfort to the group experience. Additionally, the increasingly developing sense memories of an experience of comfort and security will constitute a valuable therapeutic resource for the individual client.

Former group clients of the author have reported that they can sometimes relax when under stress simply by "remembering group." Since therapy groups often deal with emotionally charged problems, the importance of a reliable context of security and comfort within the group cannot be overemphasized as a crucial condition for success with chronic and other clients.

A series of anecdotes or metaphors can be told to a group of clients over a period of days or weeks. If the metaphorical anecdotes or stories symbolically incorporate the general form of the difficulties experienced by the clients who comprise the group, the therapist can simultaneously address a variety of client issues.

In a group setting the therapist can assume that therapy with one client in the presence of others will be taken by the other clients as a symbolic metaphor for their own issues on an unconscious level. Therefore it is really not such a large step for the therapist to remain aware of the various clients' issues while speaking to one client. The therapist can then comfortably and naturalistically insert indirect therapeutic suggestions, appropriate metaphors and acknowledgments directed toward the unidentified listening clients while simultaneously respectfully attending to the needs of the identified client.

In some cases the client himself will provide a story that metaphorically represents the circumstances of several other clients. The therapist's direct work with this sort of true story will often constitute a valuable symbolic therapeutic metaphor for other clients. The therapeutic value of the story can be enhanced by meaningful looks from the therapist to appropriate clients and questions from the therapist designed to make the content of the story self-referential to the clients. Indeed some of the most effective metaphors the author has encountered have been generated by clients.

Case Example
Cazimir: Utilizing a Client's Repetitive Storytelling as a Therapeutic Metaphor for the Group

Cazimir was a 50-year-old man suffering from the effects of being institutionalized for ten years and then deinstitutionalized. He had come to the United States from Poland a decade before. Because he spoke no English he was misunderstood and assumed to be mentally retarded when he was found half-frozen and starving in a city street. Old hospital records indicated that he suffered from alcoholism. He had been recently discharged from a nursing home setting where he had spent most of the past ten years.

Like many other chronic clients, Cazimir frequently engaged in repetitive storytelling, seemingly as if on some level he hoped that if he could tell the same tale enough times the meaning and the pain attached to that meaning might somehow be transformed. If Cazimir had told this story once, he had told it 300 times! This time, the therapist recognized the therapeutic value of the story and decided to intervene to assist Cazimir and his fellow clients in discovering and utilizing the therapeutic resources inherent in the story.

In the group session, the therapist emphasized metaphorical messages to the clients by alterations in voice tone and speech rhythm. The therapist's indirect metaphorical messages to the group as a whole and to various individual members of the group are designated in capital letters in the following transcript:

Cazimir: When I was growing up in Poland we often didn't have enough to eat. I came from a family of 11 children. I was the oldest. At one time during a revolution we had only three pairs of shoes between the four brothers. My mother barely had enough food to put in the pot at night. We never knew for sure where our next meal was coming from.

Therapist: What sorts of things did you find to eat?

Cazimir: Well, sometimes just some potato peels boiled in water to make a thin broth with maybe some kind of old, dried-up carrots. I really know what poverty is like.

Therapist: That's right (*slight pause*) . . . and there are a lot of ways to be poor, ways that A PERSON SOMETIMES FINDS HIMSELF EXPERIENCING A SENSE OF POVERTY in his life. (*Therapist looks meaningfully at Cazimir and then at other clients.*) What I am especially interested in right now (*looks at Cazimir, gestures gently with open left hand toward client who recently lost medical assistance monthly benefits and is currently having trouble finding a job*) is how you FIND A WAY TO SURVIVE that sort of experience and somehow found and are continuing to LOOK FOR WAYS TO GET WHAT YOU ARE NEEDING.

In your case, Cazimir, you obviously found food, maybe not a lot and probably not especially delicious but enough to survive until you could somehow get enough money together to get over to a new country where somehow THINGS CAN BE DIFFERENT FOR YOU NOW. And by the way, how are you feeling right now in terms of rich and poor?

Cazimir: Right now I feel kind of rich in that I have all these people around me. I'm not alone like I was on the boat coming from Poland . . .

(At this point he begins to look around the room, making eye contact with the various other clients, a woman who recently lost her husband, a client who recently was kicked out of her boarding house living situation and has returned to live with relatives and feels unwanted there, and a client recently laid off from a factory job. His eyes finally come to rest on Marilyn, the client who recently lost her medical assistance benefits.)

Therapist: Would you be willing to take the opportunity right now to share some of your rich and poor feelings with some of these other people?

Cazimir: Yea . . . (*looks at Marilyn and pauses*) I feel like you really know what I'm talking about feeling really poor back then and even now in some ways and how good—rich—it is how much I need sometimes like this to be with other people, friends. I feel like you really understand.

Marilyn: I know what you mean. I feel really poor right now, in a money sense . . . but I'm feeling hopeful that I can make it even though it's really hard right now . . . if I keep on trying to get a job, maybe trying some new places, eventually I'll find one. And that, the feeling that I can make it . . . is my rich feeling. . . .

UTILIZING THE NATURALISTIC RESOURCES OF THE GROUP

In working with clients in the group or milieu group setting, the therapist is often provided with powerful therapeutic resources in the context of ongoing relationships between clients in the group. Sometimes the most effective utilization of available therapeutic resources in group settings depends on the therapist's ability to not interfere with the process of a naturalistic intervention. The following two case histories will illustrate.

Case Example
Harold: Utilizing Peer Responses

Harold was a 30-year-old married man who had, by all accounts of his employer, his wife and friends, become suddenly and unaccountably suicidally depressed. He was brought to a psychiatric day hospital program as an alternative to inpatient psychiatric hospitalization. Since he was financially successful, with a happy marriage and many friends, it was difficult for the other group clients and, initially, even for the therapist to imagine what had led to Harold's obvious despair and acute self-rejection.

For the past 10 years, Harold had been a leader of boy scout troops and a fund raiser for his church. He had a beautiful house he had built himself with his wife. He loved the outdoors and often went camping with his wife and friends where he enjoyed active hiking, boating and water skiing. Asked what was wrong, Harold would only reply cryptically, "I'm no good . . . because of what I done before." Asked if he wanted to talk about what he'd done, Harold always refused to talk about it.

In group sessions, other clients repeatedly asked Harold, "Why are you so down on yourself, why are you so depressed?" The answer was always the same: "I'm no good . . . because of what I done. I don't want to talk about it."

The response of the other clients was initially to badger Harold and try to get him to tell them what he had done in the past that was making him feel so terrible now. For weeks they tried to get him to talk. Finally, after about six weeks, everyone in the group gave up and just accepted Harold the way he was.

In the meantime, Harold had interacted with the clients on other levels. He was one of the few clients who owned his own car and was always ready to offer a ride home to anyone who needed it. Sometimes he provided transportation to job interviews and classes. Everyone in the group had grown fond of him.

One day a new group member came and again the subject of

Harold's past came up. Before Harold could reply with his usual reference to being "no good . . . because of something I done," one of the other clients intervened. He said, "Leave him alone! He doesn't want to talk about it. Besides," he added emphatically, "if he doesn't want to talk about it, it must not be important." Harold started to cry. He said, "But it is important, that's the whole problem." One of the other clients said, "If it was important you'd be willing to talk about it." Another client added, "I'm so sick and tired of this whole conversation, even if you wanted to talk about it, I wouldn't want to hear about it, whatever it was. It's in the past, man, and the past doesn't matter. What is now, your life now is what really matters."

Harold drew a quick tense breath and said anxiously, incredulously, "You really believe that?" The other client answered with obviously strained patience," Of course I mean it! I don't give a shit what you done in the past! I'm goddamn sick and tired of hearing about it! The PAST DOESN'T MATTER. IT'S OVER. What matters is your life now, what's happening now."

At this point, Harold's face became blank, his eyes glazed slightly as if he were searching, scanning something deep inside himself. He asked once again, softly, wonderingly, "You really mean it, the past doesn't matter?" The other client, impatient, replied emphatically, "Really. The past doesn't matter. Get on with your life, man." Harold repeated softly, "The past doesn't matter . . . " He sat more quietly than usual for the rest of the day as if he was deep in thought.

The next day Harold appeared in excellent spirits. By the end of the week he said he was ready to go back to work. In group, the clients were curious. They asked, "How did you get to feel better when you never talked about your problem? We never did figure out what was bothering you, anyway . . . but I'm glad you're feeling better." Harold said, indicating the client who had told him that the past didn't matter, "He did it. He made me feel better. He made me realize something important and now everything is all right. The past really doesn't have to matter. It's now that counts."

Harold subsequently returned to work. A few months later he dropped into the day treatment program to say hello and to let everyone know that he was doing fine. A year and a half later he was seen by the author on the street and stopped to say, "Everything is just fine" and that he and his wife had just become parents. To date his work and social life continue to go well.

Harold's treatment file disclosed that he had, in fact, been in therapy 14 years previously at age 15. This was followed by treatment between ages 17 and 20 as part of a probation agreement. Severely physically and emotionally abused in his family of origin, Harold had "broken down" at age 15. He had raped and robbed an elderly woman who apparently reminded him of the mother who had abused him. His teachers, neighbors, family and friends were shocked and horrified. Nothing in Harold's previous behavior had given them any indication that he was capable of that kind of act. He was sentenced to two years in a juvenile detention center. Upon release, he received therapy as part of the probation agreement for the next three years.

By all indications from his records and behavior in the community, Harold had succeeded in rehabilitating himself in the best sense. However, at age 30, upon contemplating having his own child, he began to have thoughts about his own childhood and adolescence. He was haunted by memories of his wrongdoing and was unable to forgive himself for the atrocity that he had committed. At this point he had become suicidal and, providing that he survived, was at risk for becoming a chronic client.

Individual therapy had been unsuccessful in enabling Harold to resolve his feelings about the past. Because of the risk of suicide, Harold was admitted to the day hospital program to provide support and structure during the day, with his wife providing support and caring at night. Since he was unable to talk about his problems directly, group therapy was of little avail until another client successfully accepted Harold's limits and then communicated with him on a deep feeling level that transcended the content of the problem.

It is debatable whether a therapist could have accomplished this intervention as simply and effectively as Harold's peer did. However, the most important point of this intervention is the fact that the other client's response was given in a context of deep acceptance and honest concern, and constituted a realistic observation.

Effective therapeutic interventions are not necessarily limited to the realm of trained professionals! Often the effectiveness of a given intervention depends more on the nature of the relationship between the therapist and client than on the credentials of the therapist.

Before ending the discussion of utilization in groups, it should be recognized that the community itself functions as the client's larger, ongoing "therapy group." Peers, friends, teachers, employers and virtually any caring and accepting person in the community are potentially capable of administering a naturalistic therapeutic intervention! The fact that such interventions may be deliberate or merely inadvertent on the part of the lay therapist should not prevent the therapeutic value from being recognized and appreciated.

Sometimes the competence of an Ericksonian therapist resides in the ability to recognize the therapeutic value of a naturalistic intervention when it is occurring and to resist the inevitable temptation to interfere or interrupt! All relationships with people in the community are potentially valuable therapeutic resources for the client.

The potential therapeutic value of naturalistic community interventions is illustrated in the story of Joe, in which Erickson describes an extremely brief but powerfully effective therapeutic intervention that was administered to a chronic resistant client by a peer of the opposite sex. Based on past behavior, Joe could be described as suffering from a "character disorder." However, this in no way interfered with the effectiveness or lasting quality of the intervention!

Joe had been leading a life of theft and violent behavior since age 12. Reformatory school, two prison sentences, and time in solitary confinement had not changed his behavior. After his most recent stay in prison, he returned to his hometown (also Milton Erickson's hometown) and began stealing and threatening the local people as he had in the past. One afternoon, an attractive and sought-after farmer's daughter named Susie came into town on an errand. Joe stepped in front of Susie and boldly asked, "Can I take you to the dance next Friday?" Susie said coolly, "You can if you're a gentleman." Joe stepped out of her way. The next morning the merchants in the town were surprised to find boxes of stolen goods returned.

Joe soon acquired honest employment and married Susie a year later. He became a pillar of the community, was elected president of the local school board, and thereafter led an honest and productive life (Zeig, 1980).

About this case, Erickson said, " . . . And all the psychotherapy he received was, 'You can if you're a gentleman. . . . ' All he needed was a simple statement."

This story illustrates the fact that, "Psychotherapy has to occur within the patient, everything has to be done by the patient and there has to be motivation. . . . You try to understand what your patient is telling you. Your patient has an experiential language all his own and it is different from yours" (Gordon & Meyers-Anderson, 1981, p.168).

Given adequate support and treatment that utilizes ALL available resources, there is the potential for all "chronic" and "resistant" clients to lead less constricting, more adaptive and rewarding lives. For the therapist who helps these clients along the way, and for the clients themselves, Ericksonian utilization truly offers a "path with a heart."

13

The Therapist as an Instrument

In all therapeutic endeavors, but particularly in working with chronic and resistant clients, the therapist is his or her own best instrument. This chapter focuses on discussion of the therapist and co-therapist roles in an Ericksonian perspective, what to do when the therapist feels "stuck," and specific techniques for enhancing the therapist's comfort and creativity when dealing with especially difficult clients.

Milton Erickson rigorously and continuously trained himself as a psychotherapist. He used all aspects of himself in this endeavor, including the range of his voice, his unique nonverbal communication abilities, and his personal interests. His wide range of interests and curious attitude allowed him to find common ground when speaking to virtually any client (Zeig, personal communication, 1984).

Being a therapist allows little opportunity to hide who you are. In this sense being a psychotherapist has some close similarities to being a parent (sic: apparent—no pun intended!):

You know, when it comes time for them to leave and move out on their own it's kind of awe inspiring and not a little bit scary to see all the things they picked up from you—mannerisms, values, things they do because you did them while they were around you; things they don't do because you did them and they don't want to mimic you, and vice versa. They pick up so many things that you're not even consciously aware of yourself and yet when you see them doing certain things, you recognize where that particular bias or issue or attitude came from . . . it's kind of scary, because there really is nowhere to hide even if you would want to . . . because in spending that time with you, what they pick up and respond to most is the essence of WHO YOU ARE AS A PERSON, the way you look and act. What you say or tell them to do seems to have a much lesser impact than the actual kind of person you are. (parent of two children aged 18 and 22)

The above statement, although originally voiced by a parent, is also descriptive of the therapy relationship. Despite the most conscientious efforts to be objective, the therapist cannot help but implicitly communicate some messages to the client about who the therapist is as a person.

Clients sometimes take from the therapeutic relationship things that surprise the therapist. For example, the author was recently amazed when a client told her that she had decided to learn to do needlepoint because, "after all these weeks looking at that needlepoint picture that hangs in your office, I really felt that I should try it, too."

The client's selection of implicit messages to take in can occur with or without the therapist's awareness. This situation is not unlike that of the poet who writes what she thinks is a simple poem, and is later astounded to hear all the deep meanings that are ascribed to the poem by others. The difference, of course, is that the poet can defer responsibility for the impact of her product on others—the responsible psychotherapist cannot.

Because of the nature of the therapy relationship, everything that the therapist says or does constitutes a potential implicit metaphorical message to the client. This occurs regardless of whether specific verbal communication is focused directly towards the client, or indirectly, "in front" of the client.

THE POWER OF IMPLICIT ASSUMPTIONS

One of the most powerful attributes of Erickson's work was the optimism that he communicated to clients by his way of being in the world (Rosen, 1982).

It is crucial that the therapist maintain a confident attitude and an expectation of success. The therapist's attitude regarding the therapeutic endeavor will inevitably be communicated to the client and will have a powerful influence. This perhaps accounts for the dramatic success occasionally achieved by "naive" student interns who radiate enthusiasm and hopefulness in working with chronic and resistant clients.

Therapists who feel jaded, cynical or demoralized should not overlook the resource inherent in the refreshing attitudes of students and colleagues new to the field. Eat lunch with a student!

CONSIDERATIONS FOR THE THERAPIST WHO ENCOUNTERS A RESISTANT CLIENT

All behavior is symptomatic of the problem the client brings to therapy (Erickson, 1965). Rather than constituting a rejection of the therapist, it is part and parcel of the client's symptom and should be regarded as such. Realizing this will avoid many difficulties and will allow the therapist to sidestep many of the power struggles that can potentially handicap competent therapists who wish to avoid failure.

When a client is resisting, it means that some part of the client is not feeling accepted or understood by the therapist, or in some way is fearful of engaging with the therapist. The client also may be feeling angry at the therapist or at a person whom the therapist symbolizes. The most effective way for the therapist to utilize his own feelings of frustration and confusion is to learn more about the client on a process level.

When the therapist encounters resistance from a client there are several parameters that are worth examining. If the therapist is feeling particularly upset, frustrated and angry at the client, it is likely that the client has somehow tapped into one of the therapist's own ongoing issues. This need not be viewed as an insurmountable problem, or even a difficulty that requires long hours of psycho-analysis! Instead, it should be viewed for what it is, an unsolicited but nevertheless valuable opportunity for personal growth.

Is the Client Utilizing the Therapist's Issues?

Just as the therapist can utilize anything the client does or feels in the interest of therapy, the chronic resistant client is likely to utilize anything the therapist is doing and feeling as a way to con-tinue to maintain the problem!

The therapist must remember that chronic clients are skilled utilizers in their own right. If the therapist has any particular fears, foibles, preferences, or inevitable ongoing issues, sooner or later the client is likely to tap into these. Chronic and resistant clients appear to do this instinctively. Here are some examples:

A colleague of the author was a very attractive woman. However, she had a few light facial hairs which sometimes made her feel very self-conscious. Clients would invariably mention these to her at sen-sitive moments in therapy. Characteristically, she would become flustered and forget the issue at hand. Finally she had the hairs removed.

The author wrestles with a tendency toward overweight. Despite a healthy diet and regular exercise, at times of holidays and celebra-tions a "spare tire" forms quickly around her middle. Some clients are quick to notice this and utilize it to move the focus of therapy away from them and onto the therapist! A simple admission of, "You're absolutely right, I have gained weight, and I'm working at losing it again," generally serves to settle the question and return the focus to the therapeutic issues.

If a therapist is fearful of violence, a chronic client may well sense this and act out in a more threatening manner than usual. A ther-apist who does not get along with her mother will somehow eventually attract a client who is a mother who does not feel treated fairly by her daughter! The therapist who hates yelling will tend to get clients who ''resist'' by yelling; the therapist who has trouble hearing soft voices will meet up with clients who speak incredibly softly. The list can go on and on.

One of the ways that a chronic client becomes and remains chronic is by effectively resisting the therapist. In this current age of increasingly sophisticated therapeutic training technology, one of the most effective remaining ways that a client can successfully continue to resist is to use the therapist's personal Achilles' heel. Many chronic clients seem to do this intuitively and with surprising accuracy.

A sense of humor is indispensable in dealing with the above and other similar issues from life that the client may utilize in an attempt to rescue both client and therapist from painful or difficult aspects of the client's difficulties. Following that, a simple, honest answer and a gentle but straightforward invitation to ''return to the business at hand'' will generally suffice.

Exploring the Therapist's Associations

Sometimes, the client inadvertently brings up the therapist's negative associations by symbolizing another person in the therapist's past or present. If the therapist finds himself feeling emotions that appear to be unwarranted or excessive toward the client, the therapist should explore the question, ''Who, if anyone, does this client resemble behaviorally or physically in my personal life?''

Discovering and exploring these resemblances is valuable for two different reasons. In some cases, the therapist's exploration of the client's resemblances will provide valuable clues to the client's personality traits.

In other cases, the client's physical or behavioral resemblances may explain the therapist's difficulty in relating well to the client. For example, if the client physically resembles the therapist's rejecting fifth-grade teacher, the therapist may have to reacknowledge and further integrate some old feelings that surface about the teacher. The gift contained in these old associations can be unwrapped by the therapist asking the question, ''What can I learn about myself and others from this past experience?''

Working through those old feelings will enable the therapist to feel clear in the present in relationship with the client and in many cases will in and of itself spontaneously change the manner in which the client responds.

Clients respond strongly to nonverbal cues from the therapist. If the therapist has an issue with the client, it is sure to show up in the therapist's facial expression, tone or body language, and the client will respond accordingly. That is why it is crucial that the therapist be willing to consistently work through any personal unfinished business that a client elicits. A willingness to do this not only assures the therapist of less trouble in working with difficult clients, but practically guarantees the therapist's continued personal growth and integration.

Some Methods for Working Through the Therapist's Issues

In some cases the client may bear an unfortunate resemblance to someone the therapist personally dislikes. One way for the therapist to reduce the risk of these negative feelings affecting the client is for the therapist to identify and focus on one particular positive characteristic about the person the client resembles. The association will then be of a more positive nature.

Another tack is for the therapist to identify the offending characteristics about the person and then explore in detail how these characteristics are in some way also present in the therapist. While this is a very effective method for inducing growth and constructive change in the therapist, this technique requires personal bravery and willingness to risk. This is not a strategy for the fainthearted!

Another useful option is for the therapist to engage in a Gestalt dialogue with the person whom the client resembles, expressing fully all resentments and appreciations that are felt. This experience will help clear away some of the old associational ''cobwebs,'' and will often lead to a valuable new learning.

Role Playing

With particularly difficult clients, the therapist can often learn new and valuable information and insight about what it's like to be the client by role playing the client and having a co-therapist role play the therapist. The act of identifying with the client in and of itself will frequently lead to insights that at least make the client's resistant behavior more understandable and therefore less frustrating to the therapist.

Speculating on Behavioral Resemblances

On the other hand, if the therapist notices that the client is ACTING like that fifth-grade teacher, the therapist might consider how that client might be feeling that is similar to how the fifth-grade teacher felt.

For example, as an adult the therapist knows that the grumpy fifth-grade teacher taught a class of 55 unruly students and most likely felt overwhelmed and overburdened, needing help in organizing her time efficiently and getting all the work done. The teacher's apparent mood improved when an aide was sent in to help her. The therapist's association of the client with the teacher is in this case a potential resource clue for the therapist. It is likely that the client is in fact experiencing feelings similar to those expressed behaviorally by the therapist's fifth-grade teacher. The therapist will do well to explore the possibility that the client is feeling overwhelmed and overburdened, in need of an "aid."

Speculation as Therapist Training Activity

Milton Erickson trained himself to generalize accurately from minimal information about the client through speculation. For example, he would sometimes first read only the client's presenting problem, and based on that problem speculate as accurately as possible on the client's social history. He would then write down his hypothesized history and check the client's file to see how accurate he had been in his guesses.

Alternately, Erickson would read only the social history section of a client's file and then speculate about the presenting problem. He would write down his hypothesized presenting problem and then check the file to see how accurate he had been in his hunch. In this manner he trained himself to derive very accurate information from minimal clues (Zeig, personal communication, 1984). The above strategy can well be employed by current therapists who wish to sharpen their observational skills.

WHAT TO DO WHEN THE THERAPIST FEELS STUCK

In a therapy situation, the process occasionally seems to be decidedly unproductive, and yet there is no readily apparent way to change things. The therapist has already tried everything he or she can think of and the process is not changing. Examples include situations in which an agitated client is becoming increasingly threatening, a psychotic client is perseverating in painful associations, a sleepy, depressed client appears to be withdrawing more and more, and similar instances.

In the above situations, the therapist needs to find a way to momentarily relax, shift internal gears and create a climate that allows a new therapeutic response to be created. In order to accomplish this, the therapist must find a way to interrupt his own as well as the client's current patterns. There are several simple and effective ways to do this.

Shifting Quickly to a Deeply Relaxed State: The Relaxation Cue

A valuable resource for any therapist is the ability to become deeply relaxed, albeit focused and alert, at the drop of a hat. A simple and effective way to do this is for the therapist to develop this ability outside of the therapy situation, establishing an associational cue that automatically elicits this state. The therapist's state of relaxed, focused alertness will enable her to respond efficiently and creatively in highly stressful therapeutic situations. It is also likely to improve and prolong the therapist's health. The author believes this ability is indispensable for therapists who work with chronic and resistant clients.

How to develop a relaxation cue.

1) The therapist arranges for an hour or more of uninterrupted solitude and uses a favorite relaxation method to become deeply relaxed.
2) She then identifies and focuses on a remembered or imagined situation that elicits feelings of deep security and confidence, exploring this situation as vividly as possible, focusing in great detail on the sights, sounds, and feelings. A pleasurable trance state has now begun to develop.
3) When an optimum level of relaxation, comfort, and security is reached, the therapist reaches over with one hand and, in a precise and particular manner, touches the other hand on a particular and easily identifiable place. A gentle squeeze on the wrist seems to work well for most people.
4) Subsequently, the therapist can elicit the state of deep relaxation, comfort, and security by repeating the associational cue of the gentle squeeze on the wrist.

Strengthening the relaxation cue. Repetitions of this technique will serve to refine and strengthen this associational cue for relaxation. Later, in stressful situations, the therapist can simply provide himself with the gentle wrist squeeze or other selected associational cue. This will serve to automatically elicit the desired state of relaxation whenever needed (Bandler & Grinder, 1979).

Testing and refining the relaxation cue. The above cue can be further refined with the assistance of willing colleagues. The therapist should take some time first to identify what kinds of client behaviors tend to make him feel a degree of discomfort or anxiety that leads to a "stuck" feeling. The therapist then asks a colleague to role play the problematic client behavior as vividly and accurately as possible. The therapist then gives himself the relaxation cue and experiences the change in the effect of the role-played client behavior. Often this is a very powerful experience for the therapist (S. Gilligan & P. Carter, personal communication, 1982).

Repeated several times, the above technique will result in the client's difficult behavior triggering a relaxed rather than anxious state in the therapist! The therapist will then be able to respond to the client in a far more effective and creative manner, while also experiencing much less fatigue at the end of the workday.

Potential difficulties and how to resolve them. One potential difficulty with the relaxation cue is that the therapist might attempt to use this cue before it has been sufficiently strengthened by repetition. If the relaxation cue is not strong enough, it will "collapse" in the face of extreme behavior from a difficult client. If this occurs, the therapist simply must again elicit the relaxed state, perhaps using slightly different associations, and practice it a number of times. The more vividly the therapist images the sights, sounds, and feelings that constitute the experience of the state of security, comfort, and relaxation, the more effective this technique will be.

A new touch (kinesthetic) cue can then be introduced to trigger the relaxation state. At this point, the therapist should arrange to test the cue by having colleagues role play difficult client behavior. Once the therapist is confident of the strength of the relaxation cue, it can be effectively used with clients and in other stressful situations such as public speaking, performance, etc. If the therapist is unsuccessful in developing a reliable relaxation cue, effective assistance can be obtained from another therapist who is trained and experienced in Ericksonian hypnotherapy techniques. The author urges the therapist to develop this very relaxing and useful ability to relax automatically in the face of stressful therapeutic situations.

Simple Behavioral Strategies for the Therapist Who Feels Stuck

When feeling "stuck" during a therapy session, the first rule is to change what you're doing!

First, stop for a minute and take several deep breaths. Not only will this serve to relax the therapist, it is likely to have a similar effect on the client. Then change something that you are doing. Any one of the following will generally suffice:

If sitting still, move in some way.

If moving, change something about the way you are moving or stop moving.

If talking, alter tone, volume, speech rate, or speech rhythm. Shift body posture.

Become silent if talking.

If silent, begin to speak.

Change the mood of the therapeutic communication: if loud, soften; if the communication feels impersonal, become more personal and conversational in style; if the situation feels overwhelmingly emotional, shift to a more objective tone.

Using the Co-therapy Relationship

The presence of a co-therapist provides many advantages. First of all, the co-therapists' manner of interacting with one another provides a metaphorical model which is then available to the client as a behavioral option to imitate in personal relationships.

Milton Erickson saw his clients in his home. He instructed his family not to ask the clients personal questions about their therapy, but to conduct themselves in a normal manner when the clients were present. This enabled his clients to have the benefit of observing the everyday interaction of a normal, healthy family (Zeig, personal communication, 1984).

Some similar advantages can be provided to clients by developing co-therapy situations in which the therapists demonstrate a very positive and productive manner of relating to one another.

For example, a client who has difficulty constructively handling conflict can benefit by seeing the co-therapists disagree and resolve the disagreement in a positive manner. Clients who have difficulty with intimacy may profit from observing the co-therapists exchanging a warm hello, a friendly pat on the shoulder, or a hug.

A male client who is fearful of losing his "macho" standing if he acquires domestic self-care abilities such as cooking for himself,

doing his laundry, etc., could benefit from hearing two male therapists or a male/female dyad discuss how each manages these tasks
of daily life.

Focusing resistance with a co-therapist. With a particularly resistant
hypnotic subject, Erickson spent the first 45 minutes of a therapy
session without success. He then brought in "a college girl who
was working in my kitchen" and directed the girl to go into a trance
and hypnotize the subject. Previously resistant and noncompliant,
the man immediately went into a trance for the second therapist
(Rossi, Ryan, & Sharp, 1983, p.79). With some resistant clients, the
resistance may be focused on one therapist, allowing a second
therapist to then work easily with the client, regardless of the second
therapist's comparable abilities.

The author has worked with several court-ordered referrals of
initially reluctant, angry, and resistant clients. A technique that has
been frequently successful is to allow the client(s) to focus the
resistance on one therapist and one room, and then switch to a second therapist and room.

For example, one family was referred by the social services department because the father had been accused of beating the daughter.
The father entered the author's office with the rest of the family, but
refused to sit down because he was "too damn angry to sit down."

Refusing to answer any of the author's questions, the father spent
the first 30 minutes loudly and aggressively berating the social services department, the legal system, the mental health system, the
social worker assigned to his case, the general category of social
workers, psychologists and psychiatrists, the author's "probable
incompetence," and speculated darkly about the results of coming to therapy. At this point, the author was called away on an
emergency. She apologized to the family, stating that it was necessary for her to leave. She then asked a colleague to complete the
interview, first warning the colleague about the man's ill-tempered
mood. The family moved down the hall to the colleague's office.

An hour later, the colleague came to the author wearing a puzzled
expression. She said, "He was a little grumpy at first, but nothing
like you described. He and the rest of the family answered all of

my questions and it was a very good beginning. I guess he used up all his anger and resistance with you.''

The author feels that the success of this strategy of focusing resistance on one therapist is enhanced by having the client not only switch therapists, but also change rooms. The author has also had some (although less) success when working without a co-therapist by simply using the strategy of changing rooms. Frequently, the client will ''forget'' to bring the resistance into the new room.

Sometimes, in order to enable the client to ''lose'' his or her resistance, a more dramatic change of environment is necessary. In some cases, resistance may be left in the office complex rather than just in one particular office. The therapist and client can escape the resistance by going outdoors, going for a walk in the park, or going to a coffee shop. The author once conducted a very successful therapy session with two initially resistant teenage girls in the women's bathroom! Few clients take their resistance to the bathroom with them!

Co-therapists supporting each other. Yet another advantage of working with a co-therapist is the support available to each therapist. During a difficult session, the co-therapists can provide each other needed support through eye contact and discreet reminders to occasionally shift posture to a more comfortable position, pause, and take a deep breath. This will serve to help the therapist maintain a productive state of relaxed, alert, focused awareness.

Role-playing client polarities. Co-therapists have the capability to act out integration metaphors for the client. Each co-therapist acts out one of the client's related polarities in a manner that culminates in mutual harmony. Some examples follow:

With a psychotic client who occasionally lapsed into moments of lucidity, the co-therapists took the roles of ''crazy talker'' and ''appropriate talker.'' The session began with the two therapists talking comfortably and pleasantly to each other. The client was directed to talk ''crazy'' to one co-therapist and talk ''appropriate'' to the other therapist.

She was given 15 minutes to talk "crazy." The client accordingly spoke in a psychotic manner to the "crazy" talking therapist for the first 15 minutes. She then turned to the "appropriate" talk therapist and spoke lucidly for the remainder of the hour with a few asides to the "crazy" therapist. She ended by speaking lucidly and appropriately for the remainder of the session and most of the following week, with only a few "crazy" asides. The therapists' role-playing of the client's polarities had apparently created a bridge for the client between "crazy" talk and "appropriate" talk.

A client who tended to extremes of pessimism and naive optimism suffered from recurring depressions. He would make small gains in therapy and his personal life, such as asking a woman out on a date, or doing a task well at work, only to spin elaborate, overly idealistic fantasies that later left him despairing and deeply disappointed. The co-therapists accordingly began to end each session with a discussion in front of the client in which they expressed opposing views regarding the client's weekly prognosis.

One co-therapist maintained that the client was doing "fabulous, couldn't be better," while the other therapist expressed concern and wondered, "Is he REALLY getting what he needs? . . . I worry about this guy . . . " Initially, the client just listened to the co-therapists' dialogue. After a few weeks, he began to argue with them, telling them that, while they perhaps had some valid points, in fact they were BOTH wrong—things were NOT THAT SIMPLE. A few weeks later, the client successfully terminated therapy.

A client who varied between extreme polarities of extrapunitive and intrapunitive tendencies came to therapy because of difficulties with personal relationships. The co-therapists spent part of each session openly arguing about whether the client was "actually sincere in his efforts." One therapist maintained that the client was most certainly making an excellent effort and really was succeeding despite many difficulties with unsympathetic people in his life. The other therapist maintained that the client was probably fooling them both and doing little while blaming everybody else.

The client gave no visible reaction to the arguing by the therapists. In fact he acted as if it hadn't occurred. After a month, the client called one of the therapists late one night. He said, "I just had to call you, and I want to call (co-therapist), too. I got it! You don't have to do that anymore! I figured out what you're doing . . . " The client's discovery of the pattern and purpose of the therapists' role play did not elicit anger; instead it resulted in a new awareness and, eventually, a more rewarding and less constricting world view.

The above technique can be applied to any extreme polarities that are causing difficulty for the client. Crucial to this approach is the therapist's honest, congruent expressions of respect, caring, and positive regard for the client. Clients are well able to sense whether techniques are employed out of a loving concern or an impersonal posture of "experimentation." The former will elicit positive therapeutic integrations; the latter—anger and resistance. This is reasonable and understandable. As one formerly resistant client laughingly explained when the author praised her recent high grades in college courses, "We mental patients may sometimes act a little crazy, but that doesn't mean we're stupid!" The therapist would do well to remember this.

Appendix A

The paradoxical attendance contract is designed to be used in interventions in extreme cases of clients who request and apparently need therapy, but repeatedly and chronically fail to show up for scheduled appointments.

Following an unexcused absence, the client is REQUIRED to wait for AT LEAST as long as the typical (or average) number of days that he or she has characteristically stayed away from treatment in the recent past.

This requirement places the client's past behavior in compliance with the therapeutic agreement, thus providing two therapeutic advantages: 1) The formerly "resistant" client is now complying with the treatment, resulting in increased rapport between therapist and client; 2) In order to continue to "resist," it would be necessary for the client to "insist" on coming to therapy more frequently.

Client Name _____

Date signed _____

THERAPY ATTENDANCE CONTRACT

This contract is designed to ensure both that you benefit from receiving treatment and that you only schedule and attend appointments at times when you truly want to, and consequently are able to benefit from treatment. An important part of successful treatment is learning to listen to your own needs.

Therefore, each time you miss a scheduled appointment, you will be asked, as a requirement of your therapy, to wait at least ( )* days before attending your next scheduled appointment. This will ensure that you do not inadvertently attend appointments more frequently than you feel that you should, despite the views of the staff.

Date of next scheduled appointment: _____

_____

(Client Signature)

_____

(Therapist's Signature)

_____

(Signatures of other service providers or significant others)

_____

_____

Note to therapist: Insert a number based on the average amount of days client is characteristically absent from therapy following a missed appointment.

Appendix B

The purpose of the metaphor worksheet is to provide practice in constructing process-oriented metaphors for given client problem situations, and to provide the therapist with an efficient method for creating reliable and effective therapeutic metaphors to be used in actual therapy situations.

The Metaphor Worksheet

Personal background information that may be useful to incorporate in the metaphor:

(List some of client's favorite expressions, interests, experiences)

(List some of client's least favorite expressions, subjects, experiences)

Metaphorical Symbols

	ACTUAL	METAPHORICAL SYMBOL

List:

ACTUAL	METAPHORICAL SYMBOL
(1) Client's problem	symbol for problem
(2) Desired therapy outcome hope or client's hope	symbol for client's hope
(3) Client's objections	symbol for client's objections
(4) Client's motivation	symbol for client's motivation
(5) Unanticipated resource for the client	symbol for client's unanticipated resource
(6) The therapeutic change (action)	symbol for client's change
(7) Regression leading back to further integration of the therapeutic change	symbol for integration

Appendix C

The purpose of this worksheet is to assist therapists in gathering information that is useful for designing effective reframing interventions for problem behaviors.

**Reframing and Transforming Problem Behaviors
Assessment Worksheet**

(1) Describe the problem behavior.

(2) Describe setting in which the problem behavior typically occurs.

(3) Describe exact sequence of problem behavior.

189

(4) In what naturalistic situations would the problem behavior be considered less of a problem, adaptive, or possibly appropriate?

(5) List as many of the client's resources (strengths, skills, abilities, positive characteristics, good relationships, etc.) as possible:

(6) List several of the client's strong beliefs, habits, preferences:

(7) List possible small adjustments that could be made in the client's problem behavior. Speculate on how a change in any one of the following would affect the problem behavior:

duration:

frequency:

place performed:

client's attitude toward behavior:

other's attitude toward behavior:

other people's involvement (subtracting or adding):

(8) Identify as many behaviors as possible that would interrupt the problem behavior:

(9) What would be the effect of introducing some aspect of the client's resources (see #5) or strong beliefs or preferences (#6) to the problem situation?

References

Bandler, R., & Grinder, J. *Patterns of the Hypnotic Techniques of Milton H. Erickson, M.D.,I.* Cupertino, CA: Meta Publications, 1975.

Bandler, R., & Grinder, J. *Frogs Into Princes.* Moab, UT: Real People Press, 1979.

Beahrs, J. O. *Unity and Multiplicity.* New York: Brunner/Mazel, 1982.

Berensen, B., & Carkhuff, R. *Teaching as Treatment: An Introduction to Counseling and Psychology.* Amherst, MA: Human Resource Development Press, 1967.

De Shazer, S. *Patterns of Brief Family Therapy, An Ecosystemic Approach.* New York: Guilford Press, 1982.

Dilts, R., Grinder, J., Bandler, R., Delozier, J., & Cameron-Bandler, L. *Neuro-Linguistic Programming I.* Cupertino, CA: Meta Publications, 1979.

Erickson, M. H. Self-exploration in the hypnotic state. *Journal of Experimental and Clinical Hypnosis, 3,* 1955.

Erickson, M. H. Naturalistic techniques of hypnosis—Utilization techniques. *American Journal of Clinical Hypnosis,* 1958, *1,* 3–8. In E. L. Rossi (Ed.), *The Collected Papers of Milton H. Erickson, Vol. I.* New York: Irvington, 1980.

Erickson, M. H. Further techniques of hypnosis—Utilization techniques. *American Journal of Clinical Hypnosis,* 1959, *2,* 3–21. In E. L. Rossi (Ed.), *The Collected Papers of Milton H. Erickson, Vol. I.* New York: Irvington, 1980.

Erickson, M. H. "The surprise" and "My friend John" techniques of hypnosis: Minimal cues and natural field experimentation. *American Journal of Clinical Hypnosis,* April 1964a, *6,* 293–307. In E. L. Rossi (Ed.), *The Collected Papers of Milton H. Erickson, Vol. I.* New York: Irvington, 1980.

Erickson, M. H. An hypnotic technique for resistant patients: The patient, the technique, its rationale, and field experiments. *American Journal of Clinical Hypnosis,* July 1964b, *7,* 8. In E. L. Rossi (Ed.), *The Collected Papers of Milton H. Erickson, Vol. I.* New York: Irvington, 1980.

Erickson, M. H. The use of symptoms as an integral part of therapy. *American Journal of Clinical Hypnosis*, 1965, *8*, 57–65. In E. L. Rossi (Ed.), *The Collected Papers of Milton H. Erickson, Vol. I*. New York: Irvington, 1980.

Erickson, M. H. The interspersal technique for symptom correction and pain control. *American Journal of Clinical Hypnosis*, January 1966, *8*, 198–209. In E. L. Rossi (Ed.), *The Collected Papers of Milton H. Erickson, Vol. II*. New York: Irvington, 1980.

Erickson, M. H. The varieties of double bind. *American Journal of Clinical Hypnosis*, January, 1975, 143–157. In E. L. Rossi (Ed.), *The Collected Papers of Milton H. Erickson, Vol. I*. New York: Irvington, 1980.

Erickson, M. H., & Rossi, E. L., *Hypnotherapy*. New York: Irvington, 1979.

Erickson, M. H., & Rossi, E. L. From a taped dialogue, 1973. In E. L. Rossi (Ed.), *The Collected Papers of Milton H. Erickson, Vol. IV*. New York: Irvington, 1980a.

Erickson, M. H., & Rossi, E. L. The indirect forms of suggestion. In E. L. Rossi (Ed.), *The Collected Papers of Milton H. Erickson, Vol. I*. New York: Irvington, 1980b.

Erickson, M. H., & Rossi, E. L. *Experiencing Hypnosis*. New York: Irvington, 1981.

Erickson, M. H., Rossi, E. L., & Rossi, S. K. *Hypnotic Realities*. New York: Irvington, 1976.

Erickson, M. H., & Zeig, J. K. Symptom prescription for expanding the psychotic's world view. In E. L. Rossi (Ed.), *The Collected Papers of Milton H. Erickson, Vol. IV*. New York: Irvington, 1980.

Gordon, D., & Meyers-Anderson, M. *Phoenix*. Cupertino, CA: Meta Publications, 1981.

Grinder, J., Delozier, J., & Bandler, R. *Patterns of the Hypnotic Techniques of Milton H. Erickson, M.D., II*. Cupertino, CA: Meta Publications, 1977.

Kramer, E., & Brennan, E. P. Hypnotic susceptibility of schizophrenic patients. *Journal of Abnormal Psychology*, 1964.

Proust, M. *Swann's Way* (C. K. Scott Moncrieff, trans.). New York: The Modern Library, 1928.

Rosen, S. *My Voice Will Go With You: The Teaching Tales of Milton H. Erickson*. New York: W. W. Norton, 1982.

Rossi, E. L., Ryan, M. O., & Sharp, F. A. (Eds.) *Healing in Hypnosis*. New York: Irvington, 1983.

Watzlawick, P., Weakland, J., & Fisch, R. *Change: Principles of Problem Formation and Problem Resolution*. New York: Norton, 1974.

Whitaker, C. *The Evolving Therapy of Carl Whitaker*. New York: Guilford Press, 1982.

Zeig, J. K. Hypnotherapy techniques with psychotic inpatients. *American Journal of Clinical Hypnosis*, 17(1), 56–59, 1974.

Zeig, J. K. (Ed.) *A Teaching Seminar With Milton H. Erickson*. New York: Brunner/Mazel, 1980.

Index